World Peace

A Fantasy?

By

Oluwafemi Akinkugbe

Dedication

I dedicate this book to my parents, Mr. Timothy Akinkugbe and Late (Mrs.) Elizabeth Akinkugbe. Also, to my wife, Dr. (Mrs.) Olubunmi Akinkugbe and my children Oluwafemi Jr., Oluwadamilola, and Oluwafunmilayo. They encourage me to keep working until the goal is accomplished. Above all, to God be the glory.

Contents

Chapter One:
Introduction

The term peace holds tremendous power. By definition, peace means being in a place devoid of hatred, where each corner is filled with respect, care, and love. In such a place, the conflicts are peacefully handled.

Interestingly, peace is a human right, and everyone has the right to exercise it.

Revising the Definition of Peace

Peace as a term is often used frequently, but it is also elusive to define. We often approach it via our binary thinking. For instance, war and peace are often used together, which means either war exists or peace.

However, we must understand the premise of negative and positive peace and its implications to understand peace thoroughly.

Negative Peace

This is a different way of looking at peace.

It means the absence of conflict/violence in a certain place. Interestingly, it is not entirely wrong, as the Global Peace Index shows that sixty percent of people globally are worried about sustained serious harm from violent crime. However, negative peace presents an incomplete picture, leading to several misconceptions about establishing peace. It readily assumes that peace is attained when guns are no longer part of the equation.

This shuts down the possibility of finding new approaches to peacebuilding and development. As is the case, peacebuilding extends well beyond the confines of security and creates the conditions required to restructure societies to adapt and modify to continuously changing environments.

It fails to describe resilient peace, which does not relapse into violence and is associated with different social characteristics we find desirable—for instance, stronger economic outcomes, better well-being measures, and sustainable environmental performance.

The Global Peace Index (GPI) is an index that ranks one hundred and sixty-three countries and independent territories in terms of their peacefulness annually. The index shows that the threats in a system change all the time. The index, for instance, shows that crises and conflicts have declined in the past decade, but the pandemic added a new wave of uncertainty and tension.

Granted, some forms of violence have declined in the short term, but this was replaced with the uneasiness of lockdowns and rising economic uncertainty, leading to civil unrest and thousands of violent incidents during peak pandemic times.

Therefore, the pandemic was another indicator that became a new threat to regional and global peace in due time.

This also shows that political instability and violent demonstrations are also subject to non-war-related elements.

The Inclusion of Peace

Since peace is a fundamental human right, it must be established in all possible aspects. For instance, peace should be the cornerstone in regional politics, international trade, and maintaining peaceful diplomatic relations with neighboring and other nations.

The Addition of Peace Education in the Curriculum

For obvious reasons, it certainly makes sense to have 'peace education' in the education system. Everyone must know that peace is in itself an index that decides the economic viability of countries, just to name one thing.

Needless to say, peace is very important and deserves a separate place in the world forum. Interestingly, there is a reason World Peace Day is celebrated on the 21st of September annually.

The Necessity of Peace

People trapped in conflict zones desperately require peace, security, and a future, which are essentially basic needs.

However, it is not that easy since establishing trust, livelihoods, institutions, and relationships involves a long-term and sophisticated endeavor cluttered with steps forward and some backward.

These are the conventional challenges of a peacebuilding process, and we cannot afford not to do it.

Listed below are three reasons why peacebuilding process matters a lot:

- **The repercussions of conflict are far-reaching:** Interestingly, the people who risk everything to arrive on the peaceful shores of Europe are almost always from Somalia, Syria, Afghanistan, and other places besieged by violent conflict, political repression, and insecurity. Now, addressing the plight of the refugees is one way to resolve the matter. However, a better approach should be to initiate a strategic peacebuilding process at the 'source location.' As is the case, it will take unified and concerted efforts ranging from medium to long term before the root causes and drivers of conflicts can be dealt with.

- **Military Solutions Do Not Always Work:** Many, if not all, violent conflicts center on the issues of inequality, exclusion, and injustice. So naturally, criminality can feed onto a particular conflict, wherefore unaddressed and genuine grievances could also be at play, translating into violence. Although military power could be put to use to defend/prevent an immediate threat. However, it can work as a painkiller, which is a temporary fix but does not address the root cause. The economic, social, and other challenges will still complicate the task.

- **Conflict Upends Lives and Counters Development:** Interestingly, over one and a half billion people reside in nations torn apart by violent conflicts. Around sixty billion people are forcibly displaced globally, whereas twenty million are refugees. Children are a huge part of these refugees. Interestingly, a low-income country, amidst conflicts, has achieved UN Millennium Development Goals. Peacebuilding approaches, like diplomacy, dialogue, mediation, and participation, are necessary elements that can herald an era of peace and economic growth.

Peace is Not the Absence of War

We must first understand the causes and logic of war. Only then can we understand the true essence of peace.

Interestingly, war is not illegal per se. It is allowed in the UN Charter to prevent crimes of aggression. More so, the concept of a fair war also exists under international humanitarian law. So, sometimes, war may be necessary, even moral. Historically speaking, crimes against humanity and genocides have been concluded via the use of force.

However, the peacemaking track record of humans has been less than impressive. Over the past bygone decades, it has been difficult to come up with any armed conflicts that have truly ceased. Many, if not all, simmer or boil along periodically. For instance, there are conflicts in Kashmir and Palestine and struggles in Myanmar.

In other cases, the national authorities have often been preoccupied with persistent internal divisions, like Pakistan, which faces unrest from its tribal areas. South Sudan has seen waves of ethnic violence.

On the international front, the United Nations (UN) has invested billions of dollars and deployed thousands of peacekeeper troops in dozens of countries. Many UN envoys, alongside regional bodies like the African Union, European Union, and ASEAN, overlap war zones. Furthermore, the NGOs and think tanks are occupied, peacebuilding projects are launched, and peace conferences hosted by major personalities fill up the calendar.

Some efforts of the UN Security Council resolutions are backed on the rare occasions when the great powers think so. In such cases, sticks and carrots dangle in the form of aid inducements and sanctions of varying degrees.

However, this tried-and-failed type of peace business seldom produces spectacular returns; actually, it is far from it. The most it will do is put a temporary lid on violence as the lead characters in these events will sign any document under pressure that allows them to take a breather or regroup. This will be followed up with a peace deal or ceasefire due to a conflict that has flared up. And the cycle keeps repeating itself.

However, worse still, some concerns are often raised that premature peace meddling can prolong conflicts. This was the evidence on the ground in the case of the Korean Peninsula, Bosnia, and Herzegovina.

As is the case, conflicts only end when they are fully ready for it. Ideally, that would be when the differences/underlying causes are addressed, including justice for the wrongs perpetrated and accountability. However, reality works differently, which is why wars typically conclude when one side has won. For instance, WWI, WWII, or Vietnam ended when one side won decisively.

Why is World Peace Important?

We should dispel the pernicious myth that peace and prosperity are hopelessly unattainable and complicated. That is not true and far from the truth.

Peace and prosperity are easily attainable by offering basic freedom to all people - everywhere in the world. These freedom variants are listed below:

- Freedom of speech
- Freedom of religion
- Freedom from want
- Freedom for the environment
- Freedom from fear

Now, of course, other rights are just as important. However, these five fundamental freedoms establish a framework that can help other frameworks to thrive. If these five pillars of freedom are considered, they will become a pivotal part of our daily lives.

Usually, most people have never seen a war, nor will they experience it. For many, a war is something that is far away and movie-esque. Some may deem it as fun since they have not experienced one.

However, a war is real and poses grave and several consequences. People can lose the following post-war:

- The lives of family members (immediate and extended)
- The destruction of infrastructure
- The loss of human lives/civilian casualties

The people who survive are compelled to live a life of fear and suffering as they are surrounded by violence or abandon everything they know and are comfortable with. They must take immense risks to escape to another country while in the line of fire.

So, while this might seem distant and far away to many people living in peaceful zones, it is the standard way of life for people trapped in conflict zones.

1. The Establishment of Peace in Conflict Zones

There is a reason world peace should be the new normal. It is necessary for the well-being of civilians, stable governments, and everything that concerns the well-being of a country.

Therefore, the attainment of world peace is important, especially in conflict zones. As is the case, conflict creates much instability and fear in the areas as a war creates disaster and suffering. It also slackens the availability of resources, among other issues. The disastrous repercussions of war could be the following:

- Economic difficulties
- The lack of food and water
- The loss of lives and mass migrations from the conflict zone areas

- The lives of people who live in conflict zones must deal with the horrors of the war and the challenges that come with

To summarize, war and conflicts are realities that can be painful and complex for the ones living it daily. The short-term effects of war are nothing short of disastrous, but then the people and the governments have to tackle the long-term effects, which take considerable time to overcome.

Therefore, world peace is the ideal state of the world that should be established to prevent the aggravation of problems further on.

2. The Road to World Peace

Interestingly, world peace is the single hope humanity is left with. However, we must understand the premise of World Peace and what it encompasses.

World peace implies cooperation among countries without violence. The definition of peace is not only about the absence of war but also the presence of law and justice in a country.

The state of world peace is achieved when countries resolve their conflicts without any abuse/violence and work together to improve the lives of civilians in their countries.

Unfortunately, and interestingly, World Peace is a neglected agenda that urgently needs addressing. The acts of aggression visible during the Second World War foreshadowed the presence of the League of Nations and the Paris Peace Agreement. However, recent times also depict similar events with just different actors. The aggressors have changed, and so have the international bodies that are standing as spectators in the ensuing events.

The definition of world peace is subject to change over time as the zeitgeist determines it. For instance, just a hundred years ago, world peace would be deemed as the end of armed conflict and the substitution of armed conflicts with multilateral covenants and treaties. Today, world peace has acquired a different meaning altogether. Essentially, its ambit has increased.

Conclusion

Remarkably, believing that we live in one of the most peaceful periods in recorded human history is not easy. Homicides have fallen in most parts of the world, whereas the horrors of wars between countries have been at historic lows, too. Although the deaths in civil wars in South Sudan, Afghanistan, Syria, and Yemen cannot be entirely discounted, these deaths are still a fraction of what they have been at any time during history. The fatalities due to extremism have also declined over time, wherefore they were on the rise at one time.

Needless to say, we live in turbulent times, which means that peace can feel like a distant concept sometimes. It seems it will occur when we are no longer here to experience it. However, history says otherwise. Peace has been achieved before, and there is no reason it cannot be achieved again.

World peace can be achieved by us and us alone. In essence, we have more power than we would like to believe.

Chapter Two:
The Nature of Conflict

Conflict refers to any disagreement, friction, or discord among more than one person or a group. It comes to pass when one or more individuals resist the beliefs/actions of one or more individuals/groups. Incidentally, conflict can arise if one party perceives another party as having ideals/ideas or taking actions incompatible with the other party's interests. As this chapter will demonstrate, conflict takes on different natures and may vary in intensity.

The Nature of Conflict

How we resolve conflicts is possibly an important factor in any and every relationship. Unfortunately, many parties resolve them with basic approaches where one wins and the other loses. This approach can be harmful and ineffective to the relationship at hand. So, we must look at conflict holistically because it is slightly complex in how it shapes up among individuals, people, groups, organizations, and even countries.

1. Conflict is Process-Oriented

Interestingly, conflict is layered since it develops as such. The first layer of conflict is a misunderstanding; the other layers involve differences in viewpoints, values, interests, and interpersonal variances. It is called a process for a reason since it initiates when one party perceives the other to harbor a different view/interest that may contradict their own. As a result, it often leads to competition, collaboration, compromise, or maybe avoidance.

2. Conflicts are Inevitable

It should be no surprise that conflict can exist almost anywhere. Since the thought process of each individual varies, it can lead to interpersonal differences. These differences could be due to values or whatever, which can lead to conflict. However, conflicts can be resolved in several ways or, at worst, minimized. Similarly, they can be diverted and resolved as well. Conflict happens because people have different mindsets, backgrounds, perceptions, interests, egos, and missions. However, it is also healthy at times and shapes events better. For instance, teams often undergo a process: form, storm, norm, and perform. This raises the bar of excellence among the team members and, by extension, the team itself.

3. Conflicts are Part and Parcel of Life

Be it individuals, groups, and organizations—they all have ever-diversifying and changing needs yet limited resources. Therefore, this conflict is bound to happen at one point or the other and thus lead to conflicts. Interestingly, the problem is not the conflict here but the poor management which causes the issue.

4. Perception

Conflict only exists when one party or the other perceives it. In interpersonal interaction, perception is more significant than reality. Whatever we think and perceive also affects our communication, attitudes, and behavior. The Cuban Missile Crisis was a prime instance when two of the biggest superpowers came head-to-head with one another due to a false perception withheld at the time.

5. Opposition

Either party would harbor a perception that the other party is thinking/doing something against their interests. Conflicts usually happen when ideas/positions/actions receive opposition from the opposing parties for various reasons. This opposition could be due to a falsely held perception by either of the parties.

6. Interaction and Interdependence

Conflict does not happen in a silo. There will be some real/perceived interdependence for a conflict to happen. And there can be no interaction without any interdependence. Therefore, conflict occurs when an interaction has taken place. When there are different ideas between different people, then conflicts are bound to happen.

7. Conflicts are Omnipresent

That is correct - we may notice conflicts among individuals, groups, or organizations. Even nations would conflict with other nations. Conflicts have existed since the time when the first man arrived. From there on, conflicts have been omnipresent as human populations continued to spread over different places and span continents.

8. Conflict could be multi-dimensional

Yes. Conflicts can be multifaceted and have varying degrees of intensity and magnitude. For instance, a conflict does not happen in a silo since it carries with itself several risks, which makes it multi-dimensional. So, a conflict in one domain will affect people in different dimensions, which means it may lead to a vast number of repercussions.

Causes of Conflicts

We can use many ways to explore the nature of a conflict and identify the factors that play a role in it. Even though it takes certain triggering events to initiate an open confrontation, conflicts can be quite complex and may involve several factors that eventually culminate into one. Therefore, some distinctions are important to make and circumvent sweeping generalizations.

- Proximate/immediate cause
- Underlying cause

1. Proximate Causes

This is a cause that refers to an action/event that the law deems as the primary cause of something. In cases with multiple events, the proximate cause need not be the first or last act, as there are several proximate causes. These are those events that can trigger violence. For instance, the unfortunate assassination of Archduke Ferdinand of Austria in the summer of 1914 precipitated a war that embroiled the entire European theatre.

2. Underlying Causes

These causes can be long-term but fundamental and often unaddressed. When conditions develop on this front, it can quickly trigger and escalate the conflict. Interestingly, proximate and underlying causes are interrelated. However, during a conflict, special attention must be given to the underlying causes to establish lasting peace in the region/area under question. Explanations centered around underlying conflicts target the human agency or the social structural conditions that cause the problem(s). The focus is studying factors that come under the ambit of the 'nature vs. nurture' debate to see how events have progressed.

Sources of Conflicts

As mentioned above, conflicts can take many forms and vary in intensity. This section will explore the different sources of conflicts from which they stem and briefly examine them.

1. Information

Conflicts can arise due to variances in interpretations, information, and misinformation. It could be possible that disputants may have inadequate information or not even the same information regarding something.

Similarly, different individuals and groups could interpret the data differently or prioritize it accordingly. The situation can become complex when control over data, manipulation, and obstruction comes into play.

2. Relationship

This conflict variation occurs when personal perspectives differ from one party to the other. One party could have a skewed perception of events and could trigger conflict. Perceptions could differ based on stereotypes, rumors, and whatnot. This kind of conflict could occur in a workplace environment, sports, or even among two people since no two people are alike.

3. Values

This can occur when individuals/groups/others have differing views on the morality or ethics of something. Their perception of right or wrong could differ, resulting in a deadlock from conflict. Conflicts based on relationships and values could be subjective since they depend on how a person feels about something/someone.

4. Interest

This type of conflict occurs when a person's supposed outcome does not align with the other person's/group's interests. It happens when a person thinks that if something happens as one party hopes, their interests will be affected. For instance, two athletes are on a team but have vastly different approaches to the game, or a married couple could differ in choosing an apartment or a villa.

5. Miscommunication

This is a big source of conflict and can occur despite having no incompatibilities among the individuals/groups, yet misunderstanding and miscommunication can still occur. Secondly, stakeholders could have different perceptions regarding a situation. So, a resolution is not possible until clarity is provided. Thirdly, emotional bias, prejudices, self-interests, self-centeredness, and varying perceptions can create conflict. The lack of skill and ability to explain something or communicate with people could stem confusion, hurt, or cause anger, fueling the conflict further. The people's experience can be very real, whether the conflict is perceived or actual.

6. Resources

This can refer to conflicts over material resources, including objects, land, or money. These are commodities that are easily identifiable and negotiable. Historically, access to scarce natural resources, territorial control, raw materials, and other resources have fueled these conflict areas. For instance, the early nineteenth and twentieth centuries' colonialism was mainly a war for resources and to expand the wealth of nations that stepped out into the world. Every European country wanted to push the envelope of colonialism as much as possible, and all their actions were directed in pursuance of that goal. When push came to shove, these countries resorted to military solutions to bring the desired parties in line and protect their interests. The war for resources resulted in conflicts in different parts of the world as competing interests vied for the same resources.

For instance, major superpowers in the past have taken drastic measures to preserve their control over oil reserves in the Middle East and different parts of the world. In the same vein, colonial superpowers would exhaust resources in colonized countries to benefit their home countries. This eventually led to conflicts in colonized countries by the ruling governments, civilians, and others who saw these colonizers as usurpers of wealth and natural resources.

For instance, the subcontinent (involving Pakistan, India, and Bangladesh) led a united front against their oppressors/colonizers who had bled the subcontinent of its wealth, manpower, and natural resources. When the British left the subcontinent, it was reduced to a conflict-ridden theatre devoid of its glorious past.

The demand for freshwater, land, and other vital natural resources will become increasingly important in the coming years. This demand and struggle for resources will breed a fresh wave of conflicts in due time.

If we look at climate change, the superpowers are also in perpetual conflict. No superpower wishes to decrease its manufacture and production while playing a pivotal role in raising the carbon footprint in the atmosphere. An unwritten conflict exists between them while they vie for Earth's most prized resources.

7. Relationships

Relationships are as old as humans. However, each human being sees relationships differently. For instance, some may take a reactive approach, whereas others may take a proactive one. Gandhi would have preferred to cooperate with the opponent and build a relationship leading to a peaceful life after the conflict.

Generally, humans have different relationships at work, community, family, and other places. So, disagreements could surface in different settings, which is standard.

Sometimes, relationships could be affected due to interdependence, which could shift the power dynamics in one party's favor. For instance, a wife, a victim of domestic violence and constant abuse, cannot walk out of a bad marriage as easily since she depends on her husband for her needs. The husband is fully aware of this power dynamic and continues to exploit her wife.

Secondly, an employee wishes to leave a firm but cannot since the company is well-reputed. However, the employee knows the dynamics of the firm and finds it detestable. The company has a clear advantage in this case.

8. Interests and Needs

The lack of nonfulfillment of interests and needs could equally lead to conflict. The nonfulfillment of these interests/needs could be just a perception or a reality the person/party finds unsettling. In most cases, identity forms the foundation of many conflicts. For instance, colonized subjects will struggle for independence and an identity that has been theirs all along. Therefore, conflicts that seem to be a contest for material wealth may have an identity-based backdrop.

Conflicts can occur when the following is denied:

- Perceived/actual usurpation of economic resources and their unfair distribution to the people
- Inequality in terms of equal rights, respect, safety, and participation in the social life
- An absence/lack of cultural, identity, or religious values or their perceived threat

Structural violence occurs when individuals/groups/communities face threats in these areas. Apart from these areas, vertical structural violence can occur in the following areas as well:

- Alienation: The loss of identity
- Exploitation: Economic well-being is missing
- Repression: The absence of need is freedom

According to Gandhi, exploitation was the root cause of violence. He perceived violence as something that hindered self-realization and that violence could be structural/direct in nature.

9. Religion

As is the case, religion has fueled some of the biggest conflicts in human history. On the other hand, religion is one's private matter as it deals with inner self and spirituality on a personal level. However, the situation becomes complex when religions claim exclusivity and separate the wheat from the chaff.

Apart from that, political leaders use religion to sway the masses and control them. And in turn, they remain in power and exploit the people day in and day out. Religion is a tool to justify actions. We have seen in history how racism, slavery, and subordination of women have been misinterpreted over the course of centuries.

The major religions in the world have stemmed from century-old conflicts that remain unresolved to this day. It has also resulted in tremendous bloodshed and loss of human lives. Because of religion, we now see fundamental elements in the global arena that have an active presence, exceeding the confines of fringe threats.

The rise of fundamentalism in modern history has adversely affected nations and their civilians. It has led to the adoption of radical ideology, while the reaction also stems from the ideology's fascist elements. Henceforth, states and societies become embroiled in conflicts that seemingly have no end in sight. However, we should also remember that while religion has been used as a tool to create conflicts, it can also be used as a source of peace.

10. Rights

Rights are fundamental in every sense of the word. The violation of rights or downright denial or the elimination of such violations forms the heart of many such conflicts. Rights have different degrees, as mentioned below:

- First-generation rights: Political and civil rights are known as first-generation rights. They protect the right to life, liberty, and freedom of expression.
- Second-generation rights: These include cultural, social, and economic rights, which ensure health, food, shelter, and education.
- Third-generation rights: These refer to collective rights, especially those of marginalized and minority groups. It ensures that everyone lives a dignified life.

Some of the renowned Human Rights Conventions include the following:

- The Universal Declaration of Human Rights, 1948
- Covenant on Economic, Social and Cultural Rights, 1966
  Covenant on Civil and Political Rights, 1966
- Convention on the Elimination of all Forms of Discrimination Against Women, 1979
- Convention Against Torture and other Cruel, Inhuman or Degrading Treatment or Punishment, 1984
- Convention on Rights of the Child, 1989

Even though rights might be p in a state's constitution, minority/marginalized groups may be unable to access them as freely as they expect.

The 'powers that be' may hinder their rights depending on what works for them. Eventually, this can lead to a violent conflict. Therefore, exploring structural violence and assessing the stakeholders involved are prudent for resolving it in a timely manner.

11. Culture

Culture plays a vital role in social conflict. It is learned from society in different mediums (family, community, media, and school). So, we can assume that culture is not something that a child is born with.

However, culture is essential as it determines how society in a certain place thinks and acts and how they perceive events. Therefore, it is vital to understand the culture of a place before the root cause of a conflict is understood first so that we can solve it.

12. Ideology

This refers to the public world of politics, which can be a dark, vicious, and gritty place. Political ideologies like Marxism, Nazism, and Fascism have preset concepts about how to govern a society, regardless of how successful/failed they are.

As we know, the Cold War raged in the 1960s. The paradigm war between Russia and the USA raged as one camp was capitalistic, and the other was communist. This was a major source of conflicts between the two new superpowers during the 1960s, leading to several proxy wars and tense years between the two blocs. However, this Cold War concluded when the Soviet Union disintegrated.

13. Values

Values are greatly important to individuals and groups. They are belief systems that shape people's identities and add meaning to their lives.

However, values are as different as the people who abide by them. Incompatibility in values can always happen when people and groups with different value systems interact. Their preferences, principles, and practices can differ from each other.

Conflicts can occur (and predictably so) when people declare their value system (and everything that comes with it) superior to others.

This is where conflicts arise and may persist for some time.

And since values are perceived as a part of someone's identity, opposition to them presents an existential threat to their sustenance. As a result, defensive reactions from individuals/groups would be expected. The Islamic values in France are often a bone of contention that often plagues the nation, resulting in domestic unrest and political turmoil.

14. Governance

Governance concerns decisions that set expectations, grant power, or confirm performance. It deals with how a society is governed, the distribution of resources and use of authority in the right places, and its legitimacy in the eyes of the people under governance.

Essentially, governance involves decisions and systems with which strategies are implemented. Good governance is what an ideal government does. Politics is the medium with which they help facilitate good governance.

As is the case, good governance is prudent for the economic growth of a state/country. It helps with the eradication of hunger and poverty and sustainable development. Great governance helps make violence less probable.

If the government ensures that the rights of the people are protected, and everything is in line, then the authority is seen as legitimate. However, when governance competency is questioned, political and social turmoil will be on the cards as people rebel and start making efforts to initiate change. Violent conflicts will soon follow when these demands are unmet, and the governing bodies do not straighten their act. Therefore, governance is a vital source of conflict if not addressed in time.

15. Identity

The one question often asked during the Cold War era was which ideology one followed almost always. Now that the Cold War period has long gone, the question has changed.

Now, the question often asked is, who are you? This one question forms the basis of social and cultural identity. This identity is formed on the basis of religion, ancestry, values, institutions, and language. This evolved self diverges from the colonial powers and identities that have historically influenced its development.

The world has become more identity conscious as a sense of self and relation to the world are essential. As is the case, identity is an essential human need that provides a sense of security and meaning to people and helps them distinguish themselves from others. If our identity is lost and we cannot identify 'who we are' and 'how we can be,' we co-exist in a society with several identities existing simultaneously.

Case in point: Yugoslavia. The country felt proud when it stood up to the massive Soviet Union during the 1950s and 1960s and shaped its own system. However, as time progressed, Yugoslavia disintegrated as new nations emerged from its ashes (Serbia, Croatia, Montenegro, Slovenia, and Bosnia and Herzegovina). These countries formed since they felt their identity was more important than being a Yugoslav individual.

In this day and age, identity can take on different shapes and forms. For instance, language, religion, and ethnicity have become fault lines for conflict.

Ethnicity is also used as a tool for identity politics that shapes conflict in a given area/region. Time and again, different political underdogs and heavyweights have used ethnicity as a basis for differentiation and offered so-called protection from other groups. It also works to great effect since people form a united front on this basis, wherefore politicians secure their voting banks.

Conclusion

Human civilization was birthed with conflicts. Different tribes of humans fought to expand their power and consume resources for their tribal subjects. Tribes formed into societies, and societies formed into countries. Countries formed into continents and formed different blocs. Yet, the prevalence of conflict still prevails even today. Conflict exists at several levels—personal, group, organizational, national, and international—so people/groups are/will be in a state of conflict. However, we, as a society, have come far and have worked out ways to resolve conflicts over time. Different conflict resolution strategies work effectively in different instances.

In conclusion, humans have forever remained in a perpetual state of conflict. These conflicts may arise when more than one person is involved in a certain event/situation/place. We have come a long way (historically, economically, culturally, societally, and others). So, ways to resolve conflicts are also one too many.

Chapter Three:
Hurdles to World Peace

By definition, world peace is an idealized version of peace among people and countries on Earth. Different philosophies, religions, cultures, and organizations have differing concepts of how peace can be accomplished. Politicians, through time and age, secular organizations, and religious outfits have often broached the subject of world peace and its establishment (though their means to facilitate it can vary). The ideas thrown in this regard range from education, technology, engineering, diplomacy, medicine, and human rights.

The League of Nations preceded the United Nations (1945) to end wars that ravaged different continents. However, due to its lack of success, the United Nations (consisting of the UK, USA, China, France, and Russia) was later formed. It operated to resolve conflicts without involving war in the mix. However, the success ratio of the UN in preventing wars is still a question mark. But that is for a good reason—the achievement of peace is not as simple as it sounds. It can get way complicated upon closer inspection.

Structural Violence

Structural violence is a different form of violence that refers to social institutions and social structures that can cause harm to people as it restricts them from addressing essential needs. Interestingly, structural violence is less visible, but it is a lethal version of violence and results in excessive deaths. These deaths occur due to persistent inequality in society, which would rarely be the case in equal societies.

Therefore, the violence type can take a deadly turn since it can rise in scope and implication in contrast to other violence forms. Interestingly, it can grow exponentially when unequal power differentials lead to the creation of further unequal structures. However, people overlook this form of violence as it is entrenched within the system so well that people are accustomed to it daily. So, they are ignored as ordinary life's difficulties.

The following are the instances of structural violence that demonstrate its prevalence all around:

- Gender
- Racial disparities
- Health
- Economic
- Racial superiority

Secondly, the derivative forms of structural violence involve the following:

- Symbolic
- Cultural
- Daily violence

Structural violence is a cause of potent behavioral violence since it leads to suicides, homicides, war, and episodes of mass murder. Therefore, it should be an essential area of study in this day and age. The analysis and conceptualization of structural violence can facilitate peace research via the accommodation of conditions that help further peace holistically as opposed to steps taken merely to prevent violence and war.

Economic Inequality

Rising levels of inequality lead to economic imbalances, and in the view of productive investment opportunities, the resultant outcome is higher unemployment levels. It is imperative to promote fair and sustainable development to ensure peace. In doing so, it will do away with inequalities. As is the case, inequalities are the basis of conflict, which prevents different types of development, leaving bitter conflict in its wake.

Interestingly enough, inequality, political violence, and conflict are closely related, yet not in the way people may think. Nations with a higher rate of inequality between the rich and the poor may not necessarily experience violent conflicts compared to nations with low economic inequality. In comparison, inequalities among groups backed by religion, regional conflict, or ethnic issues are interconnected with a higher threat of armed conflict. Some good news is that identity-based inequality seems to have declined in recent times, while income inequality has drastically increased over the years.

In terms of income inequality, there never has been more inequality than before. The rising economic inequality is a worrisome factor for several reasons. However, it is not a key reason for armed conflict. The reason is that an armed conflict is rarely an individual act, as political battles are fought between groups. For instance, an armed struggle may happen between a state and a group dissatisfied for one reason or another. It could even be a fight between people who fight for an identity. So, economic inequality is not a sound reason for groups to form and rebel against the state.

Take the case of Nigeria—the nation with the highest inequality rate. Ethnic groups in the North have sky-high levels of infant mortality and subpar educational achievement than the ethnic groups present in the nation's South. Interestingly enough, fifty percent of Nigerian Christian women completed secondary education in 1980, whereas only twenty percent of Nigerian Muslim women have completed it.

There is a way to eradicate inequalities and violence. In turn, we can find peaceful and permanent solutions to different conflicts. Interestingly, local communities can lead the charge in the peace process and establish development agendas for their societies.

So, supporting local peacebuilding can start with offering sustainable solutions to conflicts and fortifying societal development. As is the case, establishing peace at the ground level is more viable than imposing it externally. It will have a lasting effect on society and the economy at large. Extreme conflict and violence have increasingly daunting effects on the national economy, resulting in lasting injustices for a few years.

Conflict-ridden areas must tackle the issue of healthcare costs, the lack of a criminal justice system, and social welfare responses. In addition, they must suffer from lost productivity and security services that could have been allocated to social spending. Therefore, promoting peaceful alternatives to violence and human rights is essential to limiting global inequality and eradicating injustice.

Power Politics

What is the implication of power politics? Let's elaborate on that in this section. International politics is as complicated as it gets, where power takes different shapes and forms. In some places, military regimes will reign supreme, while others will be under sanctions by foreign powers. Some parties would have ruled in a country for decades and hindered the emergence of other parties and so on. So, it should be no surprise that power politics forms a vital component of the international politics lexicon and international affairs.

In common use, power politics can most often carry a negative connotation. It may imply the use of coercion (the threat of using force or using force) to enforce one's will over another. As far as academic context is concerned, scholars use it in relation to international relations and history. It is generally a neutral phenomenon that outlines international politics' general traits/features. Amazingly, the semantic confusion between French, German, and English leads to different definitions and meanings of the term itself.

There are several instances of power politics in modern and ancient history. The United States is a country that has been involved in several such occasions where it puts power politics into action. In 1965, America was involved in the Vietnam War as an ally of the current Southern Vietnamese government. The main aim was to circumvent the rise of communism in this part of the world. The famed communist leader, Ho Chi Minh, was adamant about establishing a communist Vietnam that was wholly independent. America was far superior in its military prowess and resources than the Vietcong and North Vietnam combined (the latter were guerrilla forces). Secondly, America had risen to become the only superpower economically and militarily since the 1950s.

However, despite the status of America as the sole superpower on the world forum, it lost badly to North Vietnamese forces, who prevailed and won the war. Interestingly, structural power prevailed over relations and capability powers that America had on its side. The Vietcong forces used their knowledge of their areas well and picked their battles carefully against a giant. It was practically a battle between David and Goliath!

There was another issue with the strategy America had used. It wanted to eradicate communism by war, but it had not won the popular support of the local people. The Vietnamese public was not fully in tune with the capitalistic ideology America held, nor were they familiar with the American culture or its ways. The Vietnamese population was unaware of the Cold War between the Soviet Union and the USA. The war killed millions of Vietnamese civilians for something they had not internalized.

This is where Ho Chi Minh used nationalist pride and familiar culture to win the hearts and minds of his people and kept the morale high for the Vietnamese troops. Vietnam eventually won the historic war over a superpower that far exceeded it in terms of resources and whatnot.

Ideological Differences

Let's take it from the start. A political ideology is nothing but a set of opinions/values/ideas/beliefs that showcase a recurring pattern. So, any political ideology, when adopted, will compete over public policy plans and often change/explain/contest the political or social arrangements of the community/group/nation.

For instance, take the instance of the Palestine conflict. The Israeli-Palestinian conflict is a deep-seated conflict that has raged for a long time. As a matter of fact, it is a territorial dispute regarding the rights to the Holy Land. This region in the Middle East has been the cornerstone of immense historical and religious significance to the Muslims, Jews, and Christians.

The Palestinians and Israelis have contested their Holy Land rights for many years. It has become one of the longest conflicts in the world. Even though the US has supported Israel for the longest time possible, it extends diplomatic solutions to resolve the competing claims of the involved parties. As a matter of fact, many American administrations have developed and proposed peace processes to resolve the issues between the two states. The former President of the United States (POTUS), Donald Trump, implemented controversial policies restricting the two-station solution. The Biden administration revoked some of his predecessor's policies while many are still in place. The violent clashes between the two groups have reached a fever pitch.

The conflict has resulted in the deaths of millions of civilians and soldiers who have tried to grab hold of the Promised Land. The seemingly unresolvable ideological differences have resulted in a conflict that has raged for over a century in modern times and even back in the Middle Ages.

Another conflict was the separation of India and Pakistan, as the two states were formed based on two different religions. The infamous partition of the subcontinent into two countries resulted in a mass migration of people from across the countries, and thousands of casualties occurred during the migration wave. It is known as one of the world's biggest wholesale massacres due to differences in the ideology of the two leading groups (Hindus and Muslims) who struggled for a separate state against their colonial masters (the British). The partition happened at the expense of human lives and was a dark moment in both countries' history.

The Road to World Peace

As is the case, the pressures on the world are graver and expected to grow further. Therefore, humans must do away with the military habit and tackle conflict at its roots. It has caused more harm than good for the most part. Thus, constructive ways to achieve world peace are necessary to adopt. Hopefully, these ideas and strategies can herald a world that stays at peace by default:

3. Say No to Exclusion

An astounding amount of evidence shows that conflict comes to pass in places where the justice system is weak or the police are untrustworthy. In doing so, the corrupt ruling elites hamper their chances of living a good life. This is why governments must cease the stigmatization, abuse, and neglect of their people. Secondly, mass media propagation that disseminates the 'us vs. them' thinking should also be stopped as it poisons and creates a more significant divide between the commoner and the ruling elite.

4. Implement Gender Equality

The chances of conflicts (and violent ones) are likely to increase if the gender gap is massive in a country. Gender should take precedence over democracy, GDP, and ethnic-religious identity, as external and internal conflict will result in the use of force when it reaches a boiling point at some time or another. On the other hand, when women partake in the peace process, peace is highly probable to endure.

5. Equal Wealth Distribution

As per the World Bank survey, forty percent of the people who join rebel groups do so due to a lack of economic opportunities. Interestingly, relative poverty is equally imperative as societies with higher equality have greater trust and increasingly low violence levels. Economic fairness should be mandatory in public resources and taxation policies, whereas tax evasion must be discouraged. Interestingly enough, the transference of wealth (rich to poor) rather than vice versa furthers security for one and all. It does not become a cause for discontent.

6. Address Climate Change

This issue will acquire center stage in the years to come. Ecological stress due to global warming will escalate conflicts as fights over natural resources like water and land will intensify, especially in East Africa. Despite its shortcomings, the UN climate agreement presents evidence that humans can address climate change problems and mitigate the crisis before it becomes graver. Interestingly, a viable climate deal is a nice enough peace deal in itself.

7. Restrict Arms Sales

Another vital tool to herald world peace is when the sale of arms and ammunition worldwide is barred. The heavy expenditures on ramping up military capabilities can also escalate global tensions as countries preemptively arm each other to counterbalance the threat. This proliferation of arms and ammunition is what raises the threat of violent conflict and conflicts between two or more parties, whether they are neighboring nations or others.

Secondly, arms treaty signatories must respect their treaties and hold the violators of the treaty accountable. Thirdly, grave repercussions must follow for the violating parties. To further strengthen these peace treaties, turning off nuclear weapons and their developments should also be closely followed up, and their use must be made illegal moving forward. Countries that use them should expect grave sanctions.

8. More Policy Change

An in-depth study of counterterrorism, colonial wars, nation-building processes, and the war on drugs indicates a pattern of consistent failures. These policies have resulted in massive use of resources and colossal failures as it has become prevalent. Therefore, willingness and humility are necessary to repent of past aggression on the world stage for one and all. The need to make self-serving policies and counterproductive strategies should be frowned upon by all the involved parties.

9. Safeguard Political Space

The governments must allow public dissent if they wish to avoid the rise of young and marginalized groups to rise against them. In any case, otherwise, they will opt for more violent and vengeful paths, which certainly does not work for the state and its machinery. Be it across the world or political spectrum, some space must be available for people to voice their orthodox and dissenting opinions. Otherwise, repressive tools like arbitrary arrest, imprisonment based on trumped-up charges, ad hoc administrative regulations, torture, and murder can pave the way to extreme discontent among the masses or select groups.

10. Address Intergenerational Relations

Many conflicts can be deemed as youth rebellions since they take a stand against preset and established corrupt systems that have become endemic in their systems, mostly older individuals. In countries where systems are present and well set in place, the youth find it tough to voice their issues, leading them on a collision course with the ruling elite. As a result, the violence stemming from this can take on many shapes and forms, depending on the varying degree of frustration built up over time.

11. Launch an Integrated Peace Movement

One more critical tool in this regard is to promote short-lived antiwar movements that actively spread the message of peace across a nation. Countries and people need nonviolent and alternative peace processes to herald a world where peace prevails. Social movements must integrate the message of peace into their messaging. For instance, the Poor People's Campaign criticizes the war economy America subscribes to as it translates to poverty on home soil.

12. Charity Begins at Home

Peace also starts with us - citizens can also make a massive difference in the peace process. When was the last time each of us apologized for something? Think about the losing side when you win. Our wins may result in someone being marginalized, ignored, or sidelined. So, we must care about what happens to their prospects. We can also indulge in constructive conversations with people who disagree with us. The discourse will help us iron out many issues from the 'them and us' thinking paradigm, among others. As is the case, all of us can play our part in making society further peaceful and avoid sources of conflicts and injustice prevalent around us.

Conclusion

Historians may have issues with the details and how things are shaped in history. However, it is undeniable that no period in history has been without wars. For the most part, the vast extent of recorded history is cluttered with imperialism taking place on a smaller or grander scale. The mantra for empires back in the day was to use force to expand their territories and use might to acquire more land.

But then again, some periods in history have been peaceful. For instance, there were periods of peace in the Roman Empire and the long peace that ensued after the Second World War. The relatively peaceful period may have followed due to the presence of a single superpower that wielded a solid imperial influence over the world.

However, despite that, world peace seems like a bridge too far for the world to reach. Geopolitical conflicts and self-interests drive the policies of many countries even today that come at the expense of someone who is marginalized. The world will have to move on from past oppressions and extend trading ties with their neighboring nations to herald a new era of peace.

All signatories must sign and act upon a universally agreed-upon peace process. This peace charter will help facilitate dialogue and further steps that can help establish and maintain peace. Peace must be given a chance at all costs to establish a state of equilibrium and reinforce a world order that becomes the new normal for one and all.

Chapter Four:
Historical Perspective on World Peace

Interestingly, the world has never fully lived in peace. There has always been a war somewhere or the other. Few countries have avoided war for long as people wish for peace in one way or another, even those who initiate war in the first place. The peace movements start with the desire for peace, as human beings naturally tend to live in peace. It also stems from a desire of the people and governments to secure peace and reject war of any kind.

We do not see self-confessed aggressors. In the 20th century, most countries changed the names of their war department/ministry to the Department of Defense or Ministry of Defense. Interestingly enough, war has not been completely abandoned despite the emergence of the nuclear age. It is only kept below the level of global annihilation. Thus, peace movements have grown in the face of this growing violence and its threat.

What is a Peace Movement

A peace movement is a social movement that aims to accomplish ideals like ending a particular war or curbing human casualties in a certain situation. These goals often align with the establishment of world peace. Interestingly, the ideas regarding peace vary, which often results in different conceptualizations of different movements since they each stand for different ideals of peace.

13. Goals of a Peace Movement

Different peace movements can have different ideals. Basically, peace is a broad term here. As far as goals are concerned, peace movements can have one or more than one goal to accomplish. There is a sense of urgency in these movements as pressure is built over the government/entity responsible for making people dissatisfied.

Some goals of peace movements are mentioned below:

- Peace camps
- Ethical consumerism
- Nonviolent resistance
- Pacifism
- Diplomacy
- Boycotts
- Supporting antiwar candidates
- Banning guns
- Supporting transparency
- Supporting tools for open government
- Political lobbying

14. The Importance of Peace Movements

Peace movements have often been able to achieve their ends. We can look at several instances from American history where peaceful protests accomplished the goals. Several instances from American history alone make a convincing argument for a peaceful and nonviolent movement.

The 'Never again!' chant took center stage and became a major talking point, after which chemical weapons were banned following the First World War. In the same vein, nuclear disarmament led to a willful agreement never to use nuclear weapons on humanity so as not to repeat the horrors of Hiroshima and Nagasaki.

These peace activists fostered a climate that helped lead the way to nuclear arms limitation treaties. It was initiated with the test ban of 1963 and Strategic Arms Limitation treaties during the 1970s. Furthermore, American President Ronald Reagan was quick to respond to this public plea against nuclear weapons. The government caught hold of this anti-nuclear rhetoric, which was more popular among the public than the military establishments.

Peace Movements in the 20th and 21st Centuries

Interestingly, the twentieth century has witnessed the most violent wars in human history. Around twenty-five million died due to these wars, whereas many were wounded. The plague, famine, devastation, dislocation, and hardships were additional wartime repercussions that wiped off many civilians and their loved ones and ruined stable economies.

However, this same century also noticed concerted efforts to limit and prevent war, restrict arms proliferation, advance peaceful conflict resolution ideas, human rights protection, prosecute war criminals, and circumvent genocide.

These steps would lead to the promotion of peace.

This section will examine some of these concerted efforts in the twentieth century to instill peace and later in the 21st century. Efforts were underway for the promotion of peace and stability.

Famed Peace Movements in History

Interestingly, history is rife with peace efforts led by different political and nonpolitical actors with varying degrees of success and interest attached. Listed below are some of those efforts that were successful while others were not as successful.

15. Ancient Greece and Rome

Ancient Greece was a place where city-states reigned supreme instead of nation-states. Hence, these city-states were almost always in a state of war with each other. Due to this reason, many of these city-states formed an organization to limit warfare. This organization prohibited the members from cutting off each other's water supply and destroying the other. It was recognized as history's first effort to limit warfare.

Furthermore, the Olympic Games were held every four years, which additionally united the city-states. This truce established a state of temporary peace all over Greece so the games could take place without fail. No one could bear arms and commit an act of aggression during these games. Due to this reason, the peace lasted for over two hundred years or so. Interestingly, the Roman Empire extended over the length and breadth of Europe. The term known for this period is Pax Romana, as northern Africa, the Middle East, and Europe were at peace.

Interestingly enough, it was a time when no other nation was as powerful as the Roman Empire to take them on. However, the Roman Empire had some principles that united and bonded the people tightly. This greatly assisted them in maintaining an era of peace that stands as an example for others to follow.

16. The Middle Ages

The weakening of the Roman Empire led to small wars all over Europe. There was a major power vacuum that different political actors decided to fill up. This was when the church became a force for good and peace. The church custom (Truce of God) restricted fighting in private disputes during certain weekdays. The Peace of God also forbade barred fighting in holy places like shrines and churches. However, churches permitted 'just wars' like defending a church or one's homeland.

17. The Salt March

Back in 1930, Mahatma Gandhi led a peaceful protest in India in defiance of the British's new policy, which barred Indians from collecting and selling salt in the country. Gandhi walked two hundred and forty miles with the protestors as he arrived at the Arabian Sea to collect salt from the shores of the Arabian Sea.

18. The Second Hague Conference

This conference was held in 1907 in the city of Hague, which led to further conventions regarding war and provided a forum for the arbitration of international disputes. Its first conference was held in 1899, resulting in a series of conventions, declarations, and a final act to govern war and facilitate international arbitration.

19. Suffrage Parade

The message 'To ask for freedom is not a crime' still resonates today. However, this was the message behind the 1913 Suffrage Parade, which was a peaceful protest. More than five thousand women stood up for their right to political participation. This movement stands as a testimony that such movements can achieve their aims even when they are peaceful and change the system on its head.

20. The Satyagraha Campaign

Mohandas Gandhi launched this movement because the laws in South Africa made it difficult for an Indian woman to become a man's legal wife. The campaign began in Johannesburg, South Africa, and continued for many years. It vehemently protested the said Asiatic ordinance, making Indian immigration difficult in Transvaal.

21. The Versailles Peace Treaty

Soon after the conclusion of the First World War in 1918, the League of Nations was formed in 1920. Its headquarters were in Geneva, Switzerland. The Versailles Peace Treaty was signed in 1919.

The establishment of the League of Nations had little effect on global peace since many major nations did not join it. It would become a precursor to the United Nations in 1945 as the need for such a body heightened. Incidentally, the League of Nations members could not even agree with one another.

22. The Treaty of Rome

Six Western European nations signed the famed Treaty of Rome. It established the useful European Economic Community (EEC), which came into effect in 1958. The remainder of the European nations joined in later—this agreement aimed to promote economic cooperation in post-World War II and economic unity in Western Europe.

23. Paris Peace Treaty

This agreement was signed between America, North and South Vietnam, and the Viet Cong that concluded the famed Vietnam War. This accord was signed to secure peace in Vietnam and ensure the war came to an end. The agreement saw the US army and naval forces leaving Vietnamese soil for good, heralding an era of peace in the region.

24. Delano Grape Boycott

Back in the 1960s, Cesar Chavez advocated for peaceful protests and boycotts. He led a twenty-five-day hunger strike to implement legislative changes and end the willing exploitation of American farm workers. Furthermore, he led a five-year strike in Delano, California, which brought two thousand farmers to ask for minimum wage, especially for the underpaid Filipino farmworkers. The movement snowballed into seventeen million Americans boycotting American grapes, which helped unions secure good wages and security for the farm workers.

25. Montgomery Bus Boycott

In some cases, peaceful protests can bring about massive and unimaginable changes far beyond someone's imagination. This happened when Rosa Parks refused to give her seat to a white passenger on a bus in Montgomery. It stands as an instance where this plain refusal led to big changes in America. The American civil rights movement propagated the message of equal seats. This led to the US Supreme Court passing a ruling one year later in 1956, which rendered segregation on public buses unconstitutional.

26. Singing Revolution

Music and social activism can go hand in hand as well, and in some cases, they can bring desired results. Estonia did this as it sang it's out of the Soviet Union rule. The incident happened in 1988 when over one hundred thousand people gathered for five nights to oppose Soviet rule. The event is known as the Singing Revolution. In doing so, they preserved their culture while the small country held against the likes of Denmark, Sweden, and Germany, among others. Then, in 1991, the nation gained independence after decades under Soviet rule. Its population at the time of independence was only under two million.

27. The Peace Movement in the 21st Century

The hopes regarding the abolition of nuclear weapons were sky-high as the Cold War noise eventually died down. However, there is a long way to go from there. Russia and the US did agree on some bilateral reductions, and new systems were implemented to circumvent these threats.

In the case of the UK, the Trident system (the nation's nuclear program) was launched in the early 1990s; therefore, its replacement is under heavy debate at the national level. The Campaign for Nuclear Disarmament (CND) has actively mobilized public opinion and organized a massive march in the UK's history. It continues its efforts on many fronts.

28. The Role of Leadership in the Peacemaking Process

Leadership plays a crucial role in the determination and sustenance of peace. A lot is written regarding leaders, peace, and peace leadership. However, a lot less is covered about sustaining peace. A crucial trait regarding leadership for peace purposes involves cultivating qualities and attributes beyond those we ordinarily associate with individual leaders.

Leadership purposed with the sustenance of peace is described as a leader who establishes a nurturing and empowering ecosystem that unveils the positive energy and potential existing among people. It allows the people to resolve conflicts nonviolently and participate in mapping a path towards peace.

In places where people and context determine the grounds for maintaining people, leadership on this front involves facilitating inclusive and participatory mechanisms, allowing local actors to articulate their immediate needs and priorities. In doing so, they actively design and shape responses to those challenges.

Additionally, it also involves rethinking how we analyze peace and conflict contexts. This encompasses an assessment of the factors that breed violence but also takes note of the capacities that maintain and nurture peace. These delicate fault lines hold nations together despite internal and external challenges.

For instance, women, youth, and marginalized social groups deem peace differently. They also experience conflict differently than others. Therefore, specific measures must be taken in order to ensure the leadership is well aware of these varying needs and challenges.

A very important attribute of leadership to sustain peace is comprehending and leveraging polarities. Polarities should not be problematic when there is a solution in sight. It is a problem when it is not easily solvable, is ongoing, and encompasses opposing ideas. We usually deem them as dichotomies like 'peace or conflict,' 'short term or long term,' 'positive or negative peace,' and 'change or stability.' This perception to see things in stiff opposition means a failure is eventual to build a peaceful society where complex contexts exist, and challenges to peace are not always black and white.

This line of thinking has consequences. When, for instance, the relationship between peace and conflict is acknowledged in a binary way, stable societies/communities could be excluded from this assessment of peace. As a matter of fact, these are the very same societies that should be in the understudy. The cases of Senegal and Ghana, which are peaceful countries in struggling regions of West Africa, are worthy of mention.

One more powerful attribute of leadership to sustain peace is an ability to unpack the assumptions that back the thought process behind contemporary peacebuilding. This will help us better understand why concerted efforts for long-term peace eventually fail. It is imperative in a place where populism is on the rise and the nation-state is under severe stress. In such a place, international norms are contested, and emerging powers create new narratives and paradigms for how the world should work and ensure peace in the same vein.

Last but certainly not least, leadership to sustain peace must assume responsibility to cause no harm. The principle of doing no harm has been part and parcel of the humanitarian community since long before international intervention. This also includes an understanding of the efforts put in by outsiders to engineer short-term outcomes, which can herald short-term peace and stability. However, it may not always build durable peace. It may raise expectations, heighten dependence, and undermine self-organization, among several other harms.

Leadership Types for Peace

A leader striving for peace must internalize several soft skills and core traits to help them rise to the occasion and unite people behind them. This could be subjective and vary due to the challenges concerned. Listed below are some instances where leadership for peaceful purposes can come in handy:

- **Reformist Leadership**

As is the case, catastrophic events can alter the course of history. It is during this time when leaders should rise and anticipate potential disasters. We can take the example of President Mikhail Gorbachev and how he handled the Chernobyl crisis. The thing was, he realized the damage to Europe if this disaster went unchecked. It was then he realized the true danger of nuclear arsenal in human hands. He later retired Russia's nuclear warheads while the anti-nuclear movement gained ground.

The reformist leadership can begin with a simple thought or sudden clarity about things. The Russian President had that clarity and led the way. Nelson Mandela was another one who read the poem *Invictus* and knew the direction his career would take.

- **Unifying Leadership**

In-person experiences of injustice, loss, pain, humiliation, or abuse can result in continual cycles of revenge and hate. However, they can also lead to a cycle of transformation and healing. As is the case, political leaders and interest groups may often use these emotions and feelings to play people for personal and political gains. Division of people on the basis of caste, creed, religion, and cultural identities is common. Selective history, experiences, and memory can polarize people in droves.

One instance of unifying leadership is of Dalai Lama, who led by compassion, which allowed his people to gravitate towards his vision for an equal, harmonizing, and democratic world order. He introduced timely reforms, built consensus, and facilitated this unifying perspective that extended beyond national boundaries for the greater good.

- **Collective Leadership**

Imagine a scenario where someone thinks of ending violence amid a raging conflict. The accomplishment of this task is a massive undertaking and a roaring success if it eventually becomes successful. These are the times when leaders rise to the occasion and work toward a common goal.

This was how transformation took place in Liberia and South Africa, where the populace was far from united and was amidst conflict.

A group of women from Christian and Muslim communities decided to unite the interfaith community and solidarity among women. Women who were housewives, homemakers, and other professionals joined hands in this noble cause and formed an organization that fulfilled this mission.

- **Visionary Leadership**

This form of leadership encompasses the ability to view the future and foresee future obstacles and opportunities. Visionary leaders can connect the dots between the events and trends that shape up and see how this can affect the future. The leaders can see where things are headed, allowing them to make decisions similarly and align the consequent goals to achieve their desired vision.

Secondly, visionary leadership is imperative since it helps the leaders make decisions based on a clear know-how and understanding of the future. It helps them recognize the short-term and long-term goals aligned and adjust accordingly.

Take the instance of Nelson Mandela. His leadership in the post-apartheid period was a form of visionary leadership, dictating unity among all the races that had been segregated through the existing political system.

Conclusion

Looking at history, we can see that man has been in a state of war since the dawn of time. The quest for empire expansion and settling disputes has raged among mortal men for a long time. However, the need for peace has also been felt during these times. From the ancient Roman times, Middle Ages, and modern times, humans have shied away from war and its disastrous repercussions.

It shows that the world is ready to embrace peace when the right conditions are provided and systems are established to facilitate it. The development of these systems should be expedited, and binary viewpoints of complex issues should be discouraged in order to reach a wholesome solution. In doing so, we can herald a more accepting world of peace despite the complex systems in place.

Chapter Five:
Building a Culture of Peace

Conflict resolution is a part of our lives. We all face it at one time or another, whether it is our friends, work colleagues, or family members. However, that is one area of conflict—it exists in different shapes and forms. It has an individual and collective context and a political and cultural context, among many others. Take the instance when different cultures collide, resulting in different arrays of challenges, especially for the ones who are outsiders.

The Culture of Peace

The premise of the culture of peace is essentially a set of attitudes, values, behavior modes, and lifestyles that reject violence and prevent conflicts by addressing their root causes. In doing so, it resolves issues/challenges via dialogue and facilitates negotiation on individual and group levels. However, the idea well applies among nations for regional and international cooperation.

Incidentally, an education in peace is also essential to learn about nonviolence and peace, democracy, human rights, and international and intercultural understanding alongside cultural diversity. An education in peace should be organized at the grassroots level to generate awareness from the outset.

"A culture of peace will be achieved when citizens of the world understand global problems, have the skills to resolve conflicts and struggle for justice non-violently, live by international standards of human rights and equity, appreciate cultural diversity, and respect the Earth and each other. Such learning can only be achieved with systematic education for peace."

-Hague Appeal for Peace Global Campaign for Peace Education

29. An In-depth Examination of Culture of Peace

Interestingly enough, humanity direly needs a culture of peace. However, this concept is often overlooked during life's hustle and bustle, so its relevance and importance are often downplayed. A culture of peace can take a life of its own since it is founded on compassion, mutual respect, and understanding of each other. It seeks to foster an ecosystem where conflicts are resolved peacefully while equality and social justice are upheld.

Secondly, this concept recognizes that humans are interconnected. Our actions can foster a shared belief to uphold respect, understanding, tolerance, and nonviolence. Its premise demands that we transcend boundaries and embrace diversity and understanding. A world with 'a culture of peace' hopes to promote harmony and foster economic, social, and environmental justice. Not only does the absence of war matter here, but so do consistent efforts to maintain peaceful ecosystems locally, regionally, and internationally. It also understands that peace is never a static state but a dynamic process requiring constant steps in the right direction and efforts to maintain this ideal state. Failure to make invested efforts in this direction can derail a sensitive process.

The central theme of the culture of peace hugely relies on the noble belief that each individual has the power to make a difference in inching the world towards peace. In pursuance of that, people can take solid steps to advocate for peace initiatives and work to resolve conflicts. For instance, they can initiate community-based initiatives to facilitate dialogue, encourage conflict resolution, and further promote a better and deeper understanding of conflicts and social justice.

Education also plays a vital role in promoting peace on microscopic and macroscopic scales. Education must advocate for peace and raise awareness regarding the impact of violence and conflicts prevalent in society. It assists individuals in recognizing the relevance of treating people with respect and understanding and encouraging the necessity of developing empathy and compassion for others.

The culture of peace is a broad concept; it does not limit itself to individuals and groups. It is also a collective effort since it requires the involvement of civil society, governmental participation, and stakeholders. Incidentally, governments can play a vital role in promoting peace by investing in peace enforcement measures like conflict resolution, mediation, and education. Apart from the government, civil society groups can also take measures on the ground level to promote peace as they create platforms for dialogue and promote understanding and respect across the community spectrum. They can play a huge role in this regard in the short and long terms.

30. Exploring the Elements of Culture of Peace

As is the case, the culture of peace is a broad term. It involves a myriad of areas that need attention and application to implement correctly and bring about the desired results. Listed below are areas that need exploration and steady application.

- **Peaceful conflict resolution:** The elements of conflict resolution involve nonviolence, consensus building, and dialogue.
- **Respect for human rights:** An absence of human rights means no culture of peace is possible. Secondly, war and violence cannot promise the security of human rights.
- **Embrace tolerance and solidarity:** This involves the understanding that war is not a solution, as are violent conflicts. Rather, peace should be the government's de facto policy on the international front.
- **Negotiating peaceful settlements:** The threat of war and conflicts in regions and international boundaries should be a nonissue. Secondly, land mines should be

banned, nuclear weapon treaties should be enabled, and peace should ensue in regional and international conflicts. Thirdly, the manufacture of arms and weapons must be negated, and humanitarian measures must be brought into force. Post-conflict initiatives should be started by parties to maintain peace.

- **Sustainable economic growth and social development:** Efforts must be initiated to reduce the persistent social and economic inequalities. Secondly, efforts must be initiated to eliminate poverty and ensure specific benchmarks of food security, social justice, durable solutions for debt problems, and ecological sustainability.

- **Democratic government:** The elements of a democratic government involve a society free of violence, terrorist elements, crime and corruption, money laundering, illicit drugs, and a transparent and accountable government that people can support.

- **Gender equality:** The participation of women should be mandatory in all walks of life. Be it social, economic, political, or other forms, the eradication of discrimination and violence against women can move mountains.

- **Free-sharing of knowledge and information:** A culture of peace can persist for prolonged periods when information is freely available to everyone, and knowledge is up for grabs without any hurdles or censorship mandates.

Reasons for Cultural Misunderstanding: Instances

Since cultural differences are part and parcel of any society, the byproduct of these differences leads to pain and suffering. One aspect is essential to understand that a conflict situation—despite being emotionally or politically charged—may often be due to an unconscious bias regarding the cultural values of the different parties.

The differences are not always about nationality or race, as differences can be one too many (explored below). Therefore, both sides must acknowledge these differences and work out a solution to find a middle ground.

31. Cultural Barriers

This barrier hampers effective communication due to variances in ideas, practices, and cultural beliefs, among other aspects that are new to people of different cultures. No two cultures are the same, which means a myriad of barriers can spring up when people of two cultures interact. A cultural barrier may involve the following hindrances:

- Politics

- Ethnic background
- Religion
- Traditions
- Social values
- Languages
- Ideas and belief systems

32. Lack of Cultural Awareness

This cultural misunderstanding occurs when individuals from different cultures interpret a situation differently. Interestingly, misunderstanding is a standard component of interpersonal conflict. How we perceive and interpret the world is primarily a byproduct of our values, beliefs, and experiences that we have learned over time. Therefore, the imprint of culture, language, and cultural background may cause these issues to spring up.

People belonging to the same culture (and sharing the same background, language, and other cultural elements) will get along very well, so the chances of conflicts will be meager. However, a person of a different culture may not have the same privileges and conveniences as that of people with similar cultures.

33. Stereotypes

Stereotypes can be deemed as reality simplified. They often box people and cultures to a select characteristic and sideline their rich diversity. Even if many people share them, it does not make them correct or etched in reality. Stereotypes can often become a source of friction among people of difficult cultures.

34. Communication Style

Our whole lives revolve around communication. It forms the fabric of our personal and professional lives. Communication can be hindered when two people from different cultures interact, having different values and everything. Effective communication skill training can greatly assist in better understanding people and where they are coming from.

Additionally, we must figure out how to communicate with people from different cultures to form a working relationship with them. This comes with the acceptance that we come from different cultures, so their communication and understanding could differ from ours.

35. Nonverbal Communication

Communication exceeds the ambit of spoken words since our body language also communicates messages to the other person. This is called body language. The relevance of nonverbal communication has varied across the cultural spectrum. So, something considered polite in one culture could be impolite in a different culture. Smiling or making eye contact could be deemed rude in one culture, whereas it can be acceptable in another.

Therefore, we must take time to understand the other person's culture, even though nonverbal communication is easy to understand as certain body language signs overlap across cultures. However, it is essential to know the cultural contexts, too. This is because different cultures may have different understandings of body language signs.

Body language is an integral component of nonverbal communication as it can often convey a range of emotions (anger, joy, disappointment, and others). Furthermore, it also affirms whatever we say verbally.

People can wrongly believe they understand body language fluently while also deeming they send non-misleading signals. However, this may not always be the case, as there is always an unspoken threat of failing to understand body language signs properly. Additionally, nonverbal communication may involve how we dress, the tone we use, and many more cues the other person can use to decipher the message.

36. Best Recourse to Prevent Cultural Misunderstandings

There are several ways to help prevent cultural misunderstandings. One way is to learn about their cultural elements and what they do each day. Other than that, we can listen to them intently and assume less about them and where they are coming from. Other than that, their family structure, cultural values, and other elements must be under consideration.

Be sure to avoid making assumptions about how people perceive their culture. Again, it is better to understand the cultural variances of a person and where they are coming from in order to better understand how they think, feel, behave, and carry themselves in different aspects of life. Incidentally, we can find out how and where they grew up and the cultural norms prevalent at the time. These elements can vary from culture to culture and even region to region, which means that people from one similar culture can have regional variances.

Some tips to prevent cultural misunderstandings are as follows:

- Remember the power of reciprocity while dealing with people of different cultures in order to create some soft ground for a steady relationship
- Always be nonconfrontational and friendly
- Never let someone feel like they are on trial or be provocative to them
- Avoid making judgments right off the bat and rather ask for clarifications with questions
- Avoid excessive staring or laughing since it can unsettle/offend someone

In several cultures, we are expected to ask for clarification if something is poorly understood. So, if you encounter someone from a different culture you do not understand, it is prudent to clarify what they say or do to understand better. Communication is the key to resolving cultural misunderstandings.

37. Addressing the Cultural Variances

Cultural conflict can often come to pass due to misunderstandings regarding the parties' expectations, motivations, and intentions. When people from different cultures interact, these differences can spring up. Conflict management is best applied when the party understands one another's perspective about whatever is up for discussion. Therefore, prior to judging, look at the other person's perspective and where they are coming from. A basic or thorough understanding of their cultural orientations, values, beliefs, and barriers must be there to gain ground and form a working relationship with them.

This can be done by looking within and understanding how your culture differs from the other person's culture and all the elements that define your culture. Awareness of cultural differences can greatly assist in conflict resolution and allay cultural disputes. Culture is sometimes an evolving entity, meaning it can change its parameters from region to region.

Vital tips for conflict resolution:

- Assume responsibility for cultural conflict management and request the other person to do the same
- Clarify how you feel and what you need from the other individual to facilitate conflict resolution

- Never be overly critical or judgmental of what the other person says.
- Ensure you understand the other person's point of view and context and vice versa
- Listen without interrupting
- Entertain the possibility that you can be wrong and the other person could be right.
- Be open to looking at things from a different perspective

Conclusion

Lastly, we must understand that a culture of peace is no utopian fantasy. It is, instead, an essential and practical approach to establishing a better world in the present and coming years. The essential humanity factor must be understood in each individual to promote a society that reflects this overarching truth. The principles of respect, tolerance, nonviolence, and understanding can herald a world that creates a culture of peace that benefits the humanity at hand.

Granted, cultural differences may sometimes lead to conflict, but these differences should be a cause for celebration rather than conflict. Therefore, the people of the world, governments, and public/private organizations must come together to achieve this noble purpose.

Chapter Six:
Economic Democracy and World Peace

Introduction

The term democracy has Greek roots as the first word *demos* refers to citizens based in the city-states in Greece, whereas *Kratos* refers to the rule of power. In modern times, democracy has been the popular and widely spread political system globally since it considers common people and their mandates.

However, democracy is a broad term as it has evolved over time and may involve several different concepts and variations of democracy. Yet most of them are based on governance and associated methods. Economic democracy focuses on the economic well-being of the people in a country. So, in a way, this democracy aims to provide economic equality to one and all.

Admittedly, political democracy is the most popular variant of democracy as it addresses the democratic state and government and tries to control power in public sectors. However, economic democracy is slightly different, focusing more on economic power. A welfare state safeguards and promotes the social and economic welfare of the people and aspires to provide equal opportunities, wealth, and social equality distribution, forming the foundation of economic democracy.

In this chapter, we will cover the definition and origin of economic democracy, the core aims behind it, how economic democracy benefits the general public, and how it could be implemented. We will also explain the pros and cons of this concept and the policies to apply and establish a future centered on economic democracy.

The Premise of Economic Democracy

Economic democracy is a concept that has roots in Marxism and similar ideologies that focus on the worker/laborer instead of the owner/manufacturer. This system balances the economic power the state holds and supports. Secondly, it encourages the right of the active involvement of the people in the economy, irrespective of whichever social constructs and restrictive concepts people have (race, gender, class, social hierarchy, customs, and traditions, among others). The economic power is not in the hands of a few selected individuals.

Economic democracy is a variation of the economy that aims to shift the economic scales of power to the public, including consumers, suppliers, workers, and others similar to them in this lineup. The concept is a departure from the managers and shareholders who mainly function in the topmost positions of the established business structures and firms at their beck and call.

Economic democracy understands the autonomy and responsibility of an individual employee in the system. It proposes democratic reforms to allay the inequality in the system and lift the employee, enabling a greater role than before. In doing so, the inequality is driven down as the focus is more on the economic well-being of employees.

Economic democracy is by the people, for the people, and from the people. It always puts people first in every aspect of economics and management, giving them the right to work out the best course of action. In doing so, the rate of innovation increases monumentally. Secondly, every person shares the profits/losses of the business in equal parts. Resultantly, there is less economic inequality in society and the world in the same vein. However, the losses faced in business could be mitigated with the usage of collective fund reserves.

Relevance of Economic Democracy for the Population

The general public needs economic democracy more than ever, and for a good reason. It helps to take control back to the economy and assess how to run an economy moving forward. Economic democracy can help establish a sustainable economic system:

The following actions could achieve the goals of economic democracy:

- Provide the public with individual economic rights

- Allot collective ownership of the business companies
- Enabling public participation in cases of economic decision-making

Interestingly enough, economic democracy gained popularity after the infamous financial meltdown of 2007-08, making the common people lose control over their finances, alienating them and bringing the economy to its knees. Therefore, its importance can be understood in the following key areas:

38. Individual Rights

The famed Nobel laureate economist Amartya Sen defines individual economic freedom as the ability of every individual to control the economy in some shape and form. This could be attained when people have basic amenities like food, water, shelter, and clothing. This approach would uproot the inhuman conditions of the labor market, where employers would be compelled to make jobs suitable for the mass population instead of downright exploiting them.

39. Collective Ownership of Business Companies

The core premise of this concept is to provide collective ownership of businesses to the people. Economic democracy allows the people to partake in the company's decisions and so forth. In doing so, they will take ownership of the operations since it affects them as much as the profit margins and everything.

40. Public Participation in Economic Decision-making

The concept provides the power for the people to be involved in decision-making at the public level. This could mean and involve many things. They can work out how to manage resources at the macro level and stabilize the economy.

Economic Democracy: Principles

Economic democracy is a concept that strongly believes in the good and well-being of all. This is an economy where people shape policies and actions themselves, keeping their interests and rights in mind. The system frowns upon the hegemony of a select few and gives the power to people instead. The founding principles of economic democracy involve the following:

- **Principle of community:** This ensures opportunity for all since the common good of the people is hugely important. The community system takes people forward, and in doing so, no one is left behind. The system takes everyone together, and people progress to different degrees.

- **Principle of inclusion:** Economic democracy focuses on everyone's rights, regardless of color, caste, creed, race, or social denomination. Everyone has an equal right to progress anywhere and everywhere, which reduces control and opportunities to a select few people.

- **Principle of local place:** Economic democracy ensures the wealth is evenly distributed among one and all and stays local. The principle oversees the wealth distribution in a given area and, by extension, nationwide to even the prosperity scales for the people.

- **Principles of good work:** This implies labor should precede capital. The value of work done and the person doing it is integral. Economic democracy strongly believes in the people who produce good work rather than the profits generated from the work done.

- **Principle of democratized ownership:** Economic democracy establishes an enterprise design for a new era. In this system, the people contribute directly to the business and in decision-making capacities while also enjoying the profits and benefits.

- **Principle of sustainability:** This protects the sustainable ecosystem formed and maintained. The sustainability principle ensures that people benefit and that the sustainable ecosystem remains at work.

- **Principle of ethical finance:** This focuses and follows on investing and lending for people and places.

- **Principle of eradication of corruption:** This principle ensures that nobody in the system attains an unfair advantage over the others and affirms equal participation for everyone. Corrupt practice can eat up the rights and opportunities available to people, which goes against the concept of economic transparency.

- **Principle of transparency:** This focuses on achieving transparency and accountability for the proper functioning of the government and industry. If practices are not transparent, the system is unfair to many people, which can be a source of distress.

- **Principle of protection of rights:** Economic democracy acknowledges legal structures and safeguards the people's property rights. This is important as the infringement of rights could prove to be a bone of contention for many if not all.

- **Principle of abolishing hierarchy:** The concept of economic democracy eliminates hierarchical relations like employer-employee and master-servant relationships. It mainly involves all public-private partnerships like healthcare, energy, education, and financial services.

However, it must be noted that the practical implementation of these demanding principles of economic democracy is a highly grueling undertaking. While the aspect of opportunity exists for all, it can result in a bitter conflict. However, these issues could be resolved with wider societal engagement.

How to Apply Economic Democracy

It must be understood that the application of economic democracy requires actions on many fronts and work from the ground up for it to become successful. The concept changes the system on its head. Listed below are some strategies that can aid in the steady facilitation of economic democracy:

- **Prevent/Eliminate artificial market mechanisms and unethical corporate activities:** The escalation of fraudulent corporate activities like market mechanisms and lobbying can put more people at a disadvantage. Actions like artificial prices, shortages, and artificial demand can eradicate economic inequalities. In doing so, we can create a free market that can work on its own merit.

- **Money in democratic processes:** This involves the pluralist community currencies and public banking to prevent economic imbalances. The public banking and money cycle operates in a way that does not disadvantage the people and the economy.

- **Advocate for social enterprises:** Social enterprises like businesses and cooperatives founded on co-creation can provide and open up opportunities for one and all, improving the economic conditions for everyone.

Pros and Cons of Economic Democracy

Interestingly, economic democracy has many social merits. Listed below are some of these merits. However, the discussion is extensive and may cover the country's micro and macro-level aspects. In this section, we have narrowed down the core points that can bring a resonating impact:

- A workplace environment will have less hierarchy, improving the experiences of individuals, providing a sense of self-worth, and acknowledging individual contributions. This system will be individual-centric, which means people will be highly regarded.
- Companies have higher productivity when jobs are created faster in employee-centric businesses. This provides the people with an impetus to put in maximum effort since the companies work for the people rather than profits.
- Hierarchy and improved production aside, the investors find long-term interest in thriving companies. Economic democracy fosters shareholder control in the form of the long-term interests of employees. This again puts the power in the hands of the people rather than the conventional way corporate structures are set.
- Economic democracy assists with improving social relationships, which positively affects health and happiness levels. In this system, humans are prioritized over profits and system expansion. This, in turn, means social relationships will prevail over other non-human entities.
- Economic democracy curtails consumerism, which in turn promotes sustainability. This works since

consumerism targets high consumer spending and places people at the forefront and center of the economy. However, economic democracy plays down the effect of consumerism.

- Economic democracy eradicates/lessens the conflicts among public interests and the anti-democratic manipulations of international organizations that protect their own interests. This creates a system that is transparent and provides opportunities without any exceptions.

The demerits of economic democracy are far few since the system has not been applied. The system does not have a proper framework and guidelines, as even the concept is new. Incidentally, large-scale businesses and companies would be more focused on protecting their interests instead of the public ones. No proper and systematic approach exists to deal with bankrupt organizations; therefore, the taxation system in such an ecosystem is not well defined. In doing so, the promotion of economic democracy would be challenging since the concept needs to have legs to stand on its own.

Therefore, the promotion of economic democracy would be challenging in reality. The full-on implementation of economic democracy would change the parameters of social and economic growth when applied in real time. It would affect the hegemony of many established and experienced entities who have enjoyed a reign.

Conclusion

Suffice it to say—that economic democracy is a novel political system that has yet to fully form as a concept and establish its core foundation for it to become popular. The employees in this system share control, ownership, responsibilities, and decision-making to manage the resources in their communities. The concept is couched in democracy, cooperation, solidarity, and sustainability instead of profiteering and selfish interests.

The existence of economic democracy can massively curtail inequality in a society and promote higher well-being for everyone involved, particularly the working class. It also raises the shared wealth of the communities rather than allocating it to the hands of a select few.

In order to achieve economic democracy, the focus should be on shared power, partnership, and benefits for individuals rather than the creation of access to participation. Last but not least, the rising social inequalities further exacerbated due to the pandemic have paved the way for economic democracy as the need of the hour across society strata more than before. It is a novel solution that can lead to a socially equal world.

Applying this concept could be challenging since particular vested interests would mobilize against radical initiatives to make the economy democratic. As is the case, commercial interests have great resources to safeguard the status quo. For instance, they can manufacture superficial narratives similar to those opposing the concept of climate change and the threat of fossil fuel use.

However, we need a systemic overhaul, which means these forces must be overcome to address the social, economic, and ecological crises we face today if we are to benefit the global economy. Our tarnished system needs democratic mechanisms to rebalance the economic resources and decision-making from the elite one percent of the world and hand it over to the remaining ninety-nine percent of people. We must safeguard the future of coming generations, but to do that, we must overcome present challenges. Otherwise, they will be unworkable utopias rather than real-time economic systems.

Chapter Seven:
Human Rights and World Peace

Introduction: Defining Human Rights

Human rights are fundamental rights and freedoms allotted to people to which they are entitled. Some of these rights come with the territory: the right to life, liberty, freedom of thought, expression, and equal treatment before the law.

Protecting these rights is the fundamental responsibility of the government, its bodies, and other entities. These rights are inherent, which means they should not be earned or struggled with regardless of the caste, creed, race, gender, or ethnicity at hand. These are legal rights protected by the rule of law and should exist in all countries. It is conventionally deemed that military forces and governments must follow and uphold these standards. Secondly, these rights should be understood as the benchmark to formulate internal and international laws.

Incidentally, several fundamental rights should come under the violation ambit as accorded by the international human rights documents (International Covenant on Civil and Political Rights, International Covenant on Economic, Social and Cultural Rights, and Universal Declaration of Human Rights). These documents are essential as they enforce rights based on political, social, economic, and civil rights.

As is the case, human rights have always been understood and interpreted differently across human societies. However, these norms should be commonly found and should be a part of the human rights vocabulary. There is evidence of numerous countries signing these treaties and agreements, indicating unanimous agreement among the shared values. The presence of human rights norms enforces a bare minimum benchmark on the governments and other entities to maintain some degree of rights. It legitimizes the complaints of people who feel their rights are not upheld. Furthermore, these rights can be hailed as non-discriminatory and universal in nature, forming the basis for further rights and criticizing the law if their adherence becomes questionable.

Conflicts often arise when someone fails to protect human rights, leading to further human rights violations if the previous ones were left unaddressed. This jumpstarts a wave of violence that can continue for long periods. Therefore, the cycle has to cease somewhere, and somehow, because hatred engenders more hatred, peace becomes challenging. The states must devise policies centered on human rights protection to end cyclical violence. When human rights are fully protected, it leads to accomplishing peace, development, and democracy.

Despite the broad consensus on the importance and relevance of human rights and their protection by international treaties and agreements, there is a massive room for improvement even today. The nations have signed these agreements, yet the implementation and facilitation of their people are remarkably lacking. Sanctions have had a spotty track record, which means they cannot guarantee effectiveness. Naming and shaming is an avenue that can be explored.

41. Peacebuilding Phase and Human Rights Restoration

There is always a threat of suspicion and violence after a conflict. The judiciary and government institutions should bear the responsibility to maintain peace. However, governments are often complicit or weakened after a conflict has come to pass. Therefore, steps must be taken to rehabilitate war-torn societies in order to push forward. It is often argued that psychological scars often persist in the minds of civilians after a conflict as atrocities are fresh, which means reconciliation implies coming clean about past horrors and crimes. Therefore, political stability implies the safety and security of human rights and its keen management. The rule of law must be respected. Therefore, issues centered on betrayal and mistrust should be addressed, too.

The international community can also play a significant role in such unstable environments as they can ensure that former opponents will respect the agreement. The basic human rights, in theory, are the same, yet these rights should also be considered in an economic, cultural, political, and religious context. Secondly, policies must showcase contextual human rights that advocate protecting rights and avoid an intrusion into internal affairs. The local context is quite important because each nation's system, conditions, and political constraints are different.

Several psychological issues must be addressed in order to promote human rights benchmarks in post-conflict societies. Societies should launch new social norms or revive previous moral standards. Programs must be shaped to address previous injustices and allay future human rights violations. Human rights must not be a footnote in the peacebuilding and reconstruction project but instead infused throughout all the activities. Lastly, the democratization process must involve the restoration of any and every social and political right. Security, police, and military forces must be trained and briefed on respecting and adhering to basic rights.

How to Protect Fundamental Rights

There are several options and avenues to protect human rights, culminating in a peaceful and hospitable system for one and all. Listed below are these methods that could be applied on a case-by-case basis and depending on the need available:

- Safe havens should be established to protect the refugees and war victims from the violence occurring in their vicinities during an armed conflict. This strategy can safeguard the loved ones of the people and protect precious human lives.

- Firstly, peacekeeping strategies must be ratified when the armed conflict and violence begin to subside. Secondly, separate strategies should be implemented to eliminate any chances of a fresh wave of violence. These strategies play a crucial role in saving lives. A return to normalcy is only possible when peacekeeping strategies are enforced.

- Education regarding human rights should be mandatory in the general public education. Financial and technical help should be disseminated to raise knowledge about human rights. Secondly, the police and security forces should also be trained to respect and use human rights in law enforcement. Furthermore, universities and research centers must also prepare judges and lawyers in this area to avoid violation of human rights and other rights.

- Dialogue groups should be formed comprised of different ethnicities to create a trust factor. This initiative can help curtail society's fear, grief, and mistrust. A platform must be there to voice the feelings of ordinary people and humanize the enemy. An active dialogue among the victims from both sides can provide grounds for forgiveness and dialogue.

- External specialists can assist and guide the drafting of laws regarding press freedom, minority legislation, and gender equality, among other laws. These specialists can also offer assistance in drafting a nation's constitution and establishing rights on economic and political grounds.

- The perpetrators of human rights will repeat past crimes repeatedly when their activities can remain a secret. Observers, international witnesses, and reporters can pressure governments to bring the perpetrators of human rights to generate awareness and discourage waves of violence. These efforts should be made to realize the value of human life and the rights violated. Thus, effective mechanisms should be in place to address the injustice.

- A truth commission must be in place during political transitions. These commissions are independent and private bodies that investigate the human rights violations perpetrated by the predecessor and bring the perpetrators to justice quickly. This body should be independent and unbiased for a good reason. The perpetrators could be an armed militia, governmental officials, and other state and non-state actors. Thus, an international body can be set up to investigate such activities, establishing branches across different continents and countries and enabling a free flow of justice across the national and international continuum. The body should ensure that past crimes and abuses are acknowledged and fully accounted for to prevent the possibility of such incidents from recurring later.

- Furthermore, reparations for the crimes must be made to the victims of the crimes and abuses perpetrated. One more route that could be applied is for this organization to be impartial in submitting its reports to the governmental bodies for them to take action. This way, a systematic cleanup can be done.

- Despite the lack of its popularity, international war crimes tribunals should be put in place to hold the war criminals and other perpetrators of heinous crimes to bring them to justice. This move can promise and uphold human rights internally and internationally via special courts. However, the international community has often been uninterested in creating these special courts, which makes matters worse for the people facing injustices. Due to the absence of such systems and mechanisms, heinous crimes and loss of human lives persisted in Rwanda and Yugoslavia, to name a few. Similarly, the absence of this tribunal has resulted in many more war crimes committed by America and other dictators, which have remained unaccounted for decades. Granted, not all the perpetrators would be held accountable as many would escape, but it is a start. Another source of concern is nabbing the top leadership, who often approves these crimes and atrocities and remains immune to accountability. This is an area that should be well thought out.

- Several democratization measures can assist in the restoration of social and political rights. The system must have strong local enforcement mechanisms to ensure short- and long-term protection of human rights and other standards. In the same vein, a judiciary must be present in the system to provide impartial verdicts on different matters while remaining uninfluenced by the political and other markets present in the system. Free and fair elections must be prevalent in the system to ensure fair voting procedures and avoid issues due to peaceful and stable elections. And lastly, the system is finally perfect when various social structures are implemented. These social structures include higher public participation, reallocation of resources, and civil rights strengths, ensuring that all bases are covered to provide a safe and secure environment for people and governments to thrive.

- Consistent development assistance and humanitarian aid can ease the shockwaves of an armed conflict between the opposing parties. While the conflict ensues, the best recourse is to save human lives and ensure basic survival needs are met. These basic survival needs include food, sanitation, water, healthcare, and shelter. The aid should help those who have been displaced and provide rehabilitation work. Post-conflict measures should be initiated, which include reconstruction programs that can aid in rebuilding the infrastructure, economy, and different local bodies and institutions. This assistance can help the nations undergo a peaceful phase of development rather than slide into further conflicts or await gradual buildup that could take years.

Case Studies of African Countries that Established Peace

The accomplishment of peace is not exactly rocket science, as many countries have been able to achieve it. It essentially requires sincerity in policymaking and the honesty of the top leadership to facilitate these measures, which can later benefit the population and the government in tandem. Listed below are three African countries that have made tremendous strides in peace, making a convincing case that peace is possible if the intention is there:

42. Tunisia

Tunisia is emerging in the Middle East and North Africa (MENA) as a nascent democracy. This is despite the nation facing governance, security, and economic challenges with global and regional pressures in tow. Tunisia remains committed to upholding human rights and fostering an environment that can assist the citizens to voice their needs and rising challenges peacefully and freely without repercussions to their safety. This is evidenced by the healthy space available to civil society organizations and groups that voice their support/opposition and government often seeking their advice in key decision-making policies. The 2014 constitution was drafted on this footing.

Furthermore, the civil society was actively involved during the transition process. Its Tunisian National Dialogue

Quartet eased political crises and maintained the process on track. The 2011 revolution was entrenched in deep socio-economic grievances, giving impetus to civil society groups to advocate for social, political, economic, and cultural reforms that were previously neglected.

The civil society groups also proposed several additions to the 2014 constitution, including the right to work, promoting women's rights and a decent salary. Tunisia has a separate section dedicated to universal freedoms and rights, including women's rights. The new constitution goes above and beyond the rights guaranteed in the 1956 Personal Status Code. Religious freedom and rights are also protected under the law preset by the state. Lastly, a Constitutional Court promises to safeguard the rights accorded in the Constitution, whereas the power to nullify laws that go against the protection of human rights is also there.

The Tunisian parliament decreed further enforcement of women's rights in 2017, criminalizing violence against women. Additionally, the then-president formed a committee that would overlook the threat to individual rights and freedoms and investigate gender equality issues preexistent in society unaddressed by the law passed in 2017. This involved reexamining the Islamic inheritance laws, which seem lopsided and downplay a woman's share of the inheritance received.

However, Tunisia is not without its challenges since it has yet to curtail its security and economic challenges alongside unemployment woes for the youth demographic and extremist factions inside its country. There are some challenges that require addressing, but then again, many other countries have their own challenges.

43. Mauritius

The nation became independent in 1968. Successive Mauritian governments have committed to investing in human capital and establishing a great business environment to promote economic prosperity.

An investment in human capital refers to open access to healthcare, basic amenities (like water, electricity, and gas), and other basic rights. A greater level of human capital helps bring economic prosperity and development while increasing social cohesion. For instance, the free education till the university level clause in Mauritius has helped create a reliable and productive workforce while drumming up the literacy level to ninety percent, the highest level for any African country.

Furthermore, the nation provides free healthcare to its citizens while the population also enjoys a free flow of safe and clean drinking water. These strides have made Mauritius the second African country on the UN Development Program's (UNDP's) Human Development Index and sixty-fourth globally. The life expectancy is the highest compared to Africa (sixty years), whereas Mauritius boasts a life expectancy of seventy-five years.

Another pillar worth focusing on (and IEP makes a mention of it, too) is the development of a sound business environment. A market that is open and accessible to everyone for conducting business is ripe for foreign direct investment and local productions. Mauritius has policies that facilitate international and local production, supported by low tax rates, training prospects, financing avenues available, and simple administrative processes, facilitating ease of business.

When the pillars of peace are established and strengthened further, it leads to a perfect system down the line. The present facilitation provided by Mauritius to local and international businesses provides the right and fertile environment that helps businesses prosper and thrive. However, the nation is not without its challenges. It has been home to internal vulnerabilities and external pressures like trade shocks, ethnic tensions, and climate change that have affected the agricultural sector, which risks the farmers' livelihoods. Despite such massive pressures, Mauritius ranks twenty-second in the Global Peace Index, which is a great achievement.

44. Senegal

Surprisingly, Senegal has managed to secure peace in its environs, considering it is located in a region where instability and political violence are rife. Additionally, it has been home to one of the longest-running insurgency movements in the Casamance region. However, Senegal is the sixtieth most peaceful nation per the IEP's Global Peace Index (from 2017). This is a massive achievement, considering the total number of countries is above a hundred and fifty.

Interestingly, several factors account for this score. Senegal has established independent and strong institutions that oversee how power is passed around and exercised, while the constitution takes care of the rest. In doing so, Senegal has set up a stable civil society that can hold its governmental institutions accountable. The instance of the 2012 presidential elections can testify to the established law and order when one candidate attempted to run for elections a third time (despite the two-term limit in the constitution). Secondly, protests erupted in opposition to this move and successfully reversed the candidate's move to sway a third election in his favor.

Another critical factor that has ensured Senegal's stability is its ability to uphold pluralism, diversity, and inclusion. The nation's political leaders have transmitted the idea of pluralism to the population and established it as a part of its national identity, leading to an open understanding that Senegal is a diverse but unified state.

Today, Senegal is a secular nation despite ninety-five percent being Muslim. Yet, the country enjoys religious freedom and constitutional rights allotted to different people. Other than that, the country's first president was Christian, despite the overwhelming majority being Muslims, which speaks volumes about the nation's commitment to its preset values. Senegal has six official languages; therefore, its constitution prohibits forming political parties based on ethnicity and religion.

However, Senegal is not without its challenges. Despite its plural and diverse society, there have been territorial disputes in its Casamance region where separatist demands are posited. However, Senegal has opted for a non-military solution and added some moderate members of this movement to the government echelons. Also, the national language of the ethnic group has been added to the state's official languages, speaking volumes about Senegal.

Conclusion

There has been a growing consensus that international human rights laws often leave a massive room for improvement. Their implementation and successive amendments can bring about a marked change in peace, security, and economic prosperity of the nations that struggle to achieve it.

However, international organizations and related bodies can only do so much to establish peace, safety, and security in a particular country. After all, countries must also show initiative to implement policies and decisions that shape human rights for the better and herald a world where people enjoy equal rights regardless of borders and boundaries.

Mainly, people relocate due to social, political, and economic reasons worldwide. Therefore, countries struggling to provide these basic features to their citizens may experience mass migrations. Therefore, a country is what people and governments make it. So, nations struggling in this area should put their heads together and strategize on a five-year plan to curtail instability and bring peace.

Chapter Eight:
The Role of Religion in World Peace

Introduction

At its core, religion is a belief system with a preset set of practices often related to some controlling force. This entity could be a personal God or any other supernatural being. Religion may also accommodate worldviews, cultural beliefs, prophecies, texts, revelations, and morals with a spiritual meaning to the members of that faith. Religion can have mythical creatures, trances, feasts, symbols, holy places, prayers, rituals, sermons, and meditation. This is the core premise of a religion. However, religion can have different understandings as some people may see religion in one way while others may view religion differently altogether.

Religion Types

Religions are of several types. Some of these religions have acquired worldwide popularity as their followers are everywhere. However, many more religions are practiced by select populations in certain parts of the world. These religions are a little renowned to others, ranging from monotheism to polytheism and faith in different entities. The well-known religions consist of the following:

- Taoism

- Traditional African religions
- Zoroastrianism
- Baha'i
- Buddhism
- Christianity
- Confucianism
- Jainism
- Judaism
- Rastafarianism
- Shinto
- Sikhism
- Hinduism
- Indigenous American religions
- Islam

An Exploration of Conflict Due to Religion

Religion does not pose a conflict in many cases. However, select cases where religion becomes a source of conflict will be under examination in this section. As is the case, all religions are centered over a dogma (also known as articles of belief), which its followers must follow without exception and question. This can often result in intolerance and inflexibility when other beliefs enter the fray. Since it is the word of God, then how could it be compromised? However, the problem with scripture is often that its language is too vague and subject to interpretation. Thus, a conflict can arise over the right interpretation, which is often difficult to resolve due to the absence of an arbiter. Therefore, the winner in such cases is often the interpretation that entices most followers. This is where the extremist aspect of the religion enters the fray, which opens the religion to criticism regarding violence and bloodshed.

45. Religious Extremism is a Source of Conflict

As is the case, religious extremists play a role in escalating conflicts. They deem radical measures the only means necessary to fulfill the divine mission and wishes. Be it any religion at hand, religious fundamentalists often take a Manichean worldview, which posits that the world is a struggle between good and evil, and justifying with the devil is hard. Therefore, any signs of moderation could be deemed as selling and abandoning God's will.

Take the eastern and western instances of New Christian Right in America and Jama'at-e-Islami in Pakistan. These bodies have followed the local constitution but often pursue intolerant ends. In cases where moderate ways have produced lackluster results (be it social, political, or economic), the public may turn to other extreme interpretations for a solution.

Without legitimate mechanisms for religious parties to express their views, violence could be an avenue worth exploring for them. Take the instance of Hamas in Palestine and Hezbollah in Lebanon, which have engaged in violence forever. They both have an alarming number of supporters via social service work where the government is perceived as doing little to nothing for the people.

In the same vein, radical Jews in Israel, Hindu nationalists, and Sikh extremists based in India are also instances of fundamentalist movements that view an eternal threat to their faiths. This also brings the discussion topic to religious revivalism, which provides a key sense of purpose and pride to the followers, seen in many countries. Sri Lanka and Sudan are instances of this revivalism, often leading to discrimination and intolerance. Interestingly, some religious groups in Israel and Egypt hail violence as a duty. These same people do not see violence as wrong but see it as valuable and handy to achieve their ends. Furthermore, these individuals view themselves as divinely directed and thus aspire to remove any obstacle in their path.

Several religions have evangelism strains, which can cause conflicts. Believers are ordered to spread God's word and raise the numbers of their followers. For instance, the initiative to impose Christianity on people was an integral reason for the conflict regarding European colonization. Similarly, a dominant group may seek to deny the right to religion to others. This is partly to maintain hegemony over the dominant religion and minimize the feelings of inferiority complex. This is the case in Sudan and China, where suppression of China was seen. In the case of China, this is the view taken by the government as it opposes the statewide religion and makes an unwanted new rival.

These instances happen due to a sheer lack of respect for other religions and the conflict.

46. Conflict Due to Religious Fundamentalists

Another aspect of religious fundamentalism stirs when some religious individuals are disgusted by modernity. As is the case, they view the marginalization of religion in a modern society and wish to restore it to its former glory. Thus, they purify the people and religion by force and any means necessary. Interestingly, cultural globalization has fueled this trend as well. The advent of Western values and materialism has alluded to rising levels of loose morals, alcoholism, and gambling. Interestingly, this has been the official narrative of Al-Qaeda, which claims its actions are motivated by neo-imperialism and the presence of foreign military forces in Muslim holy areas.

This is not just limited to the Eastern hemisphere alone, as the Western culture is also often under attack from conservatism. For starters, Western culture prioritizes the individual over the group while questioning the role of women in modern-day society. The rise of the New Christian Right in the US voices these similar sentiments that modern society is missing out on something. The teaching of evolution in schools and abortion are select issues people feel strongly about due to losing religious traditions.

47. The Rise of Religious Nationalists

This is another area where religion is used as a tool for conflict. One instance is religious nationalists, which can give rise to extremist sentiments. These individuals perceive their religious traditions as something closely connected to their home country. Therefore, any threat to either of the two threatens their existence. In doing so, these religious nationalists often create a political party/group that protects their interests at the expense of others. Thus, the agenda will be furthered by using religious symbols despite the causes being nationalist or ethnic in origin. This was actually the case in Northern Ireland, where the Catholics adopted this strategy, as did Yugoslavia's Serbian Orthodox church and Hindu nationalists based in India.

48. The Role of Media in Marketing Religious Conflict

The advent of news media and the press has skyrocketed the usually popular and convincing portrayals of religion as a source of conflict. The worldwide media has paid massive attention to covering this area (religion fuels conflict). However, this is a case of selective perception since it is one area that induces audience attention. Not surprisingly, this same media ignores the peacemaking efforts undertaken in the name of religion.

These coverages on the perils and pitfalls of religion and the actions of religious extremists engender interfaith hostility and fear. Secondly, the media portrayals of religious conflict are often biased and one-sided, failing to inform and succeeding to inform instead. It succeeds in doing that when it misunderstands goals and alliances among groups and aggravates polarization. Throwing terms around like fundamentalist and extremist to intentionally/unintentionally mask key variances in goals, tactics, and beliefs compounds the negativity.

Religion and Conflict are Not Entwined

As is the case, no prominent religion globally has been involved in some shape or form in stirring violent conflicts in some parts of the world. For instance, religious conviction was the prime motivation for the infamous September 11 attacks in a big way, courtesy of some extremist factions operating from Pakistan and Afghanistan. In the same vein, some Buddhist monks have asserted a Buddhist identity for Sri Lanka, which can fan the flames of conflict. The case for Yugoslavia is no different either, as the Muslim and Christian leaders saw themselves as the guardians of their faiths since they defended the violence against opposing religious communities during the Balkan wars. However, there should be an awareness that there is always an inclination to make the issue more reductive than it is in most cases. Religion plays a role but is often a tool for the ruling elite and other powerful entities who aspire to achieve a particular end.

49. Iran

Iran may have particular challenges due to its Shiite clerics, but there is also underlying Iranian-Persian nationalism, which has driven the conflict for years. Furthermore, local clerics and their international policies rarely outline theological precepts or religious doctrines. Instead, it is more a case of political power usurpation and preserving the quasi-theocratic status quo.

50. Iraq

The case for Iraq is no different. The conflict between the Shiites and Sunnis rarely originates over various religious doctrines and differences but instead centers on historical and contemporary control for state power. The Shiite and Sunni identities have ethnic and religious roots; therefore, the intergroup relations are pretty similar and violent. Regarding identities, the conflict between Walloons and Flemish in Belgium or between French and English people in Canada is along similar lines, which stems from language and culture instead of religious beliefs, which remains the bone of contention.

Additionally, there is the Kurds issue in Iraq, who are ethnically in a mass majority there. These Kurds are Sunni Muslims and comprise the third principal community in Iraq. This, in any way, does not suggest that religious identity is synonymous with ethnic identity since the two are pretty different while they may have overlapping features. The lines between ethnic and religious identities are often blurred—meaning blaming one for the other and vice versa is unfair. It has been seen many times that religious identity is used to mobilize forces against one another, as evidenced in Iraq and Sudan. The population has evenly responded to these calls to action to defend the faith. Therefore, it would be reasonably wrong to misrepresent or oversimplify something when it is not the case. However, it has been a practice to do so.

51. Sudan

The nation has been home to a decades-long civil war, a religious conflict between Christians and Muslims. The north has a Muslim majority, whereas the south has a Christian and animist majority. Events took a turn for the worse in 1989 when an Islamic fundamentalist government acquired power in Sudan and aspired to Islamize all of Sudan. However, the issues between the southern and northern people extend beyond religion and seldom adopt a theological/religious shape.

As is the case, the people in the north speak Arabic and want the language to be the national language of Sudan, whereas the people in the south speak Arabic as their second or third language. The Southerners are fluent in English and thus wish it to be the national language of Sudan. Secondly, the northerners have predominantly Arabic roots, while Southerners have African roots. Therefore, racial identity is crucial and forms the basis of conflict between the South and North. So, the religious aspect does come into play, yet it overlaps with the ethnic, racial, and other geographical divisions. Religion never played a huge role in the conflict from day one. To no one's surprise, British colonialism was key in worsening these divisions between North and South for over two decades. Additionally, if religion was an issue, then Christians would not be fighting Christians, and Muslims would not be fighting Muslims.

52. Nigeria

The case of Nigeria is no less different, where religion is a divisive factor in the conflict. However, it is often exaggerated beyond proportions and touted as the leading cause of conflict. The press quickly points out that thousands of Nigerian lives have been lost due to religious warfare in the last decade. At the same time, this claim is correct since Muslims and Christians died due to riots over the Danish cartoons that depicted Muhammed. But then Christians also died over opposing the sharia court's authority in northern states. However, that makes the issue very reductive. Amazingly, the issue is more complicated since economic competition, the placement of markets, occupational differences, competition, and the ethnic identity of state officials have also played a role. This, alongside friction between migrant and indigenous populations and respect for leaders, has also fueled the conflicts.

53. Afghanistan and Somalia

The cases of Afghanistan and Somalia are closely related since the primary source of conflict is over which brand of Islam people will practice. However, the issue is further compounded by ethnic and clan-related differences between the conflict and the religious differences.

54. The Arab-Israeli Conflict

On the surface, this issue may seem over the management and access to religious sites, which often are the bone of contention and serious disagreement between Jews and Muslims. However, religion is not the most pressing factor that fuels the conflict since the underlying conflict is over the control of land and state sovereignty.

All of the abovementioned cases fully exemplify that religion contributes to conflict since it outlines identity differences, motivating conflict and violence justification. However, religion does not form the backbone of many of these geopolitical conflicts.

55. Conclusion

The motive for this above discussion was to establish that over the course of many years, religion has often not been a major factor. Yet, it is often entwined with the political, economic, and social factors prevalent in the area. Therefore, assuming that religion forms the basis of the most pervasive conflicts worldwide would be slightly unfair. Often, political, economic, and identity issues are behind such conflicts.

The Relationship Between Peace and Religion

Religion is a sore subject often alluded to as a primary indicator of worldwide conflicts. Alternatively, some have opined that religion is a strong advocate for harmony. Research initiated by the Institute for Economics and Peace (IEP) has some surprising findings—as per the research, religion is not a significant source of conflict among countries. Similarly, it does not play a defining role in hindering peace either. As per the research, religion does not play a massive role as envisioned.

The research was published in 2014 and alluded to several socio-economic factors that wield a far greater impact on peace than religion alone. The primary drivers involve political terror, gender, corruption, gross domestic product (GDP) per capita, inequality, and intergroup cohesion, which play a greater role in maintaining peace than religion. The research further shows the relevancy of these factors to have a marked impact on the global level as they drum up conflict and violence in society rather than religious beliefs.

56. The Key Link Between Peace and Religion

The only notable connection between peace and religion in the research was that high peace levels could correlate to low or high levels of religious diversity. In the same vein, moderate diversity levels result in lower peace levels, signifying the nature of the connection between religious and peace diversity.

57. Religious Plurality Enables Pacification

Some religious traits are keenly related to peace, especially the religious majority in a particular country. In their research, IEP found something interesting: Nations without any dominant religious majority tend to be peaceful and often have fewer governmentally sanctioned restrictions on religion, too.

As per this analysis, nations that do not have a dominant religious group are seventeen percent more peaceful than nations with a particular dominant religious group. These countries are, on average, twenty-five percent less religious restrictive, whereas the religious hostilities are forty percent less.

As per IEP's research, religious plurality seems to have a pacifying effect as long as there are no official restrictions. Conversely, nations with a specific religious majority will often use the state's power and access it liberally, leading to the inevitable persecution of other religious groups. This can lead to friction between religious groups and followers, resulting in an endless cycle of violence and injustice.

58. Democracies Aid Peace

That is indeed correct and proven by IEP's research. Proper democracies will almost always outperform other government types as far as the maintenance of peace is concerned.

Full-scale democracies are fifty-eight percent more peaceful, have more than a hundred percent fewer religious restrictions, and forty-nine less religious hostility than authoritarian regimes.

Interestingly, full democracies have high levels of non-believers compared to other government types. However, the general population of atheists is deficient in such democracies, which means they cannot create a marked impact to hinder peace. Further, IEP research indicates that full democracies are peaceful regardless of their environs' religious belief levels. Other than that, authoritarian regimes have been shown to harbor peace and harmony despite the religions practiced. Therefore, authoritarian regimes are the second-best performing government type, showcasing the power of enforced measures to maintain peace.

Conclusion

Even today, religion seems like a breeding ground for conflicts, and the perception has become something of the sort. However, this is not necessarily the case, as the discussion above has shown. Therefore, a crucial need is to promote a heightened awareness of the power of religion and its peacebuilding and reconciliatory role, signifying its impact. This can go a long way to resolving interfaith misunderstandings and conflicts that arise routinely. Incidentally, interreligious dialogue is also essential as it can build bridges among people of different faiths and should be furthered at different hierarchies and across different societal segments.

Misunderstandings and misinformation are overly common in the environment. It would instead help to understand other religions and push the envelope in reaching a middle ground overall. Being well-versed in different religions is good and helps clear out misunderstandings of opposing religions. This can be complemented by constructive criticism and a spirit of humility to understand and accommodate one another.

Chapter Nine:

The Integration of Science and Spirituality

The Backdrop of Science and Spirituality

Spirituality and science may seem poles apart. However, their goals are often similar, as this chapter will show. For instance, spirituality and science have both addressed the ever-eternal question of reality and truth-seeking since their inception. For starters, science's goal is to fully understand the fundamental laws and principles that govern living and non-living things. Spirituality works the same way: it deals with awakening wisdom and aspires to know the world and how people fit into this vast space-time continuum. It can be argued that science hopes to enlighten the human mind, whereas spirituality deals with awakening the heart. Each is as important as the other.

However, many still consider science in antagonism to spirituality and religion even today. The truth of the matter is that a compulsive attachment to doctrines or dogmas is quite inimical to science and exploring spirituality at a deeper level. There is some ground there since science has historically opposed religion. However, this is an area where science and spirituality do not have a discord. Similarly, the mystics of different traditions also stand in agreement. The Sufi saints, Christian mystics, and Zen masters are in harmony, although Christian and Muslim sects are often at daggers drawn for various reasons.

The twentieth-century philosopher Aldous Huxley noticed this mystical commonality across different cultures and times. In this case, there is no conflict between science and spirituality, which exemplifies the common ground that often goes unnoticed.

Interestingly and controversially, modern science is rooted in mystical traditions like the Kabbalah and alchemy. Sir Isaac Newton was arguably one of the greatest scientists ever. Yet, the man wrote extensively on alchemy, whose volume exceeds whatever work he did in science. In some ways, spirituality, science, and religion complement each other and are harmonious. Furthermore, religion was never the first to conflict with science. Instead, it was dogmatism. So, it is no surprise that dogmatism has always been the enemy of science and spirituality. And history also points in that direction since the age-old battle between science and religion is more a battle of dogma and science.

As is the case, dogma is believed to be reality itself, not just an attempt to describe reality. Similarly, alternate descriptions of reality are viewed as antagonistic and threatening. The conflicts between Christianity and science pale in comparison to the conflicts and their repercussions between Christian sects. As history remains witness, these trivial variations and understandings of fundamental dogmatic belief systems have often led to persecutions and purges in history, leaving thousands dead.

Introduction

Can spirituality and science ever go together, or are they two distinct realms with utterly no connection at all? This question has been eternally posed since the two came into inception: It is helpful to examine this hotly debated relationship to provide a deeper understanding of the world, humans, and the universe around us all.

So, how are science and spirituality related? Over the course of history, humanity has often been at sixes and sevens to understand the universe's mysteries. The two approaches that have become widely popular involve spirituality and science. Conventionally, spirituality and science are often seen as opposing forces.

For starters, science relies majorly on empirical evidence, whereas spirituality is entirely different, relying on faith primarily. However, recently, a growing consensus has given rise to the idea that these two domains may not be mutually exclusive. As a matter of fact, they could even complement one another and provide unique insights in the same vein.

Therefore, understanding how spirituality and science relate means a sound understanding of fundamental concepts. Take the case of spirituality first, which extends far beyond religious beliefs and encompasses diverse practices that aim to connect to something much greater than an individual. This connection can manifest in many ways, involving a belief in a higher power, wonder and awe at the natural world, or a person's quest for transformation and growth.

On the other hand, science works differently. It represents a systematic approach to understanding how the natural world works via observation, experiments, and forming workable theories and hypotheses. Science has remained remarkably successful in explaining various natural phenomena and driving tech-related advancements.

Spirituality can be defined as the science of 'life-giving substance.' On the other hand, physics in science studies molecular structures and atomic substructures, which are acted upon by many different forces. These forces may only define how matter forms yet fail to explain the nature of life and the composition that gives life itself. Due to such reasons, the divide between physical and spiritual sciences is still pretty big to fill.

In recent times, science and tech have remained at odds with spirituality. However, the wealth of scientific research for the past four decades establishes a somewhat convincing argument that the two could/can go together. The world is heading into a space where modern technological developments go hand in hand with psychology and medicine.

The Relationship Between Science and Spirituality

This relationship has been argumentative at best and certainly not without difficulties, as evidenced by the above discussion. Interestingly, scientifically tracking emotions is akin to searching for shapes in the clouds. This is because people's emotions vary from one person to another. However, the experience of emotions could be viewed as universal and interconnected to spirituality.

Self-transcendent emotions are the web that connects us all via prosocial behavior. Emotions such as awe, compassion, gratitude, and similar emotions connect people through the prosocial capacity. This is why transcendent emotions promote behavior that connects humans while enforcing and stabilizing the prosocial connection.

All in all, the self-transcendent emotions include gratitude, awe, compassion, appreciation, inspiration, admiration, love, and elevation. All humans will experience these emotions in one form or the other. However, most humans will undergo these emotions at different times.

These emotions help bond individuals together. Interestingly, they are linked with high levels of spirituality. And since these self-transcendent emotions focus on others, they enable meaningful and purpose-filled interactions.

As is the case, many, if not all, positive psychological interventions owe their point of origin to ancient religious and spiritual teachings, often excluded from psychopathology treatments. Therefore, it comes as no surprise that empirically valid interventions exist for the four virtues (gratitude, hope, forgiveness, and self-compassion).

Exploring the psychological theory behind these four virtues makes further strides in spirituality and science possible, which can serve more people and their vast and varying needs. This connection is an important one, warranting further exploration. Conversely, failing to explore this area could also put people at a disadvantage.

The psychology of hope was initiated in the 1950s when its explanation was couched in completing goals. In the ambit of positive psychology, it has expanded to explain how to attain goals better. The theory involves both paths to accomplish goals and agency. Hopeful thought indicates the belief that a person can find handy pathways to achieve goals and use these pathways, too. Hope, as per definition, can better the well-being and emotions of humans overall.

Based on a person's worldview, hope interventions are viable as they can find avenues to connect with the divine and improve one's well-being. It differs from one religion to another, and by understanding the agency's role in the agency of hope. So, based on that, interventions that respect the individual worldview could be more helpful and acceptable.

In the same vein, the psychology of gratitude is often conceptualized as a higher emotion related to morality. Gratitude is defined in science as a prosocial moral emotion, useful for a few reasons:

- It works as a moral barometer since it indicates/assesses when an interpersonal interaction is deemed to be beneficial
- It also shows that power is limited

Interestingly, the benefits of gratitude are pretty far-reaching, irrespective of religious ideation. It can boost a person's mental well-being by simply being thankful for whatever a person has in their life. The psychology of forgiveness has several definitions. The broadest definition implies an adaptive human instinct activated in some special social situations. By extension, forgiveness necessitates having a future relationship with someone who has slighted you in some way. In turn, it frees a person instead of the natural and knee-jerk reaction of seeking vengeance.

The works of Kristin Neff have empirically backed the psychology of self-compassion. Self-compassion conceptualized (as per the research in three key components):

- It involves expressing kindness towards oneself and addressing one's lacking/shortcomings with a nonjudgmental attitude in order to aid self-improvement and learning attitude
- Connecting one's experience of suffering with that of the collective human experience. This aids compassion for oneself and humanity in general.
- Becoming aware of suffering without being attached or making it a part of an individual's identity. This is important in order to understand suffering regardless of the contexts herein.

These four virtues of forgiveness, gratitude, hope, and self-compassion are also present in different areas of the religion. Science and spirituality overlap to accommodate the human experience and bond us collectively. Secondly, interventions that address the different viewpoints of every individual will be further impactful, as they allow for individual belief systems to be better enhanced by science.

Commonalities Between Science and Spirituality

Despite the glaring and apparent differences, spirituality and science share some common elements that can close the gap that exists between them. These elements are often overlooked due to the antagonistic nature of the two concepts and how they are viewed.

- As is the case, science and spirituality often aspire to understand how the world works. Science comprehends the natural world empirically, whereas spirituality often delves deep into the metaphysical and spiritual dimensions.

- Secondly, science and spirituality acknowledge the presence of unknowns. Science understands that its knowledge of the natural world continually evolves over time, while several areas must be explored, too. In the same vein, spirituality understands that some aspects of existence transcend human understanding and horizons.

- Science and spirituality both inspire wonder and awe. Science reveals the complexity and beauty of the natural world, where spirituality can bring about a sense of connection to something that exceeds human perception and understanding.

- The science of spirituality is an emerging field that establishes and elaborates on the relationship between these two realms. It further investigates how spirituality affects the emotional, mental, and physical well-being. Different research has showcased the beneficial effects of spiritual practices like yoga, prayer, and meditation on different health areas.

Combining Science and Spirituality

Science and spirituality can form an excellent and beneficial partnership. Much work is required to bring about the desired benefits for this to happen. Furthermore, those interested in spirituality may apply scientific law to test different hypotheses. Their mind and body can work as the testing grounds to determine the results.

59. Meditation Reduces Stress

Take the instance of modern medicine, where a whole new approach to healing has been discovered. Previously, it was generally understood and agreed that healing was possible with medicinal courses. However, the connection of mind is emerging as an alternative to medicine and gaining popularity steadily. This new area of healing contends that healing is possible via the mind and tapping the soul's power. Some notable medical institutions have begun to advocate for meditation as a viable way forward to alleviate stress and reduce stress-related illnesses. Amazingly, research indicates that people who are fond of meditation can recover from surgery than those who fail to take this route. This means that the age has come where the lines between spirituality and science are increasingly becoming blurred.

60. Yoga

Surprisingly, yoga extends far beyond the confines of the medical system. For starters, it prevents diseases, but it also covers different aspects of life, too. The accommodation of yoga and modern medicine can help the world depart from disease management to health promotion. Interestingly, the wealth of research undertaken on yoga for three to four decades has found significant beneficial effects of yoga and its correlation to happiness and health in people regardless of any walk of life. Furthermore, more work remains since yoga could benefit medicine, education, and workplace environments. This shows that science could have awe-inspiring effects on mental well-being and bring about positive effects.

Conclusion

Even today, the world is seemingly suffering. Speaking globally, people attempt to make sense of tragedy and psychological pain. From this viewpoint, the only way forward is spirituality. There is always an eternal need to expand our understanding of life's meaning, our purpose while living, and the love for humanity that we share eternally. Therefore, stepping into things that matter to humans can aid us with survival and into lives that flourish.

In doing so, all that is needed is self-compassion, love, appreciation, kindness, and gratitude so humanity can transition into a refined and better state of well-being. These are the little steps that humanity can take individually and collectively.

Interestingly enough, people seek refuge in religion when plagues hit. In the same vein, people rely on one another amid war when human casualties are piling up daily. Lastly, humans stand in hope and solidarity when terrorism takes innocent lives.

Essentially, science is an integral part of humanity. Granted, it has not explained everything. Spirituality is equally essential as it helps people wander the bigger questions. Therefore, stepping fully into the realm of science and spirituality means departing from how people show up for others and themselves. As is the case, establishing the science of spirituality into a consistent practice demands effort and intention. The benefits are far-reaching, which makes the case for its pursuance all the more necessary to the progress of the human race.

In conclusion, spirituality and science are not dissimilar and stand opposed, as many assume. Instead, they complement one another, offering distinct perspectives that ensure a comprehensive understanding of the world and the place of humans inside it.

Chapter Ten:
Conclusion and Outlook

Introduction

Humans live in a turbulent time. At times, it feels as if peace is a distant concept that can occur only when people are no longer around to experience it. However, history speaks otherwise, as peace has been achieved before and many times. In order to establish peace, the real power lies with the people, the governments, and other organizations that work tirelessly without fail to achieve peace.

The past eight decades have seen the rise of several actors actively participating in global governance. The numbers have increased like never before, seemingly highlighting that international institutions are the driving engine of social, political, economic, and policy worldwide.

The present international system involves self-help. However, there is more to that. The nations also face a prisoner's dilemma since they often find themselves challenged by the ever-expanding security challenges and competition. It is a dynamic environment where they face new challenges each year or so.

As is the case, the international community was quite unprepared to respond successfully to post-Cold War challenges, resulting in complex emergencies. Many of them revolved around cultural, religious, ethnic, or nationalistic fault lines. State and non-state actors often manipulate these lines in several cases, which have often resulted in the creation of many states. What were once hollow entities later formed into states with little attributes of nationhood, with the institutional underpinnings of legitimate governance? This is the foundation of modern-day nation-states.

As is the case, violent conflict often breaks out in a place when the agreements and fundamental ideas result in this breakdown of order. It is these agreements and ideas that regulate behavior when given the force of law and enforced by the country. Interestingly, conflict is also a political failure where the country cannot, or will not, develop political communities or enable cooperation.

The Lackluster Role of the United Nations in Peace and Global Governance

United Nations is one of the biggest institutions worldwide involved in global governance. It is a form of international bureaucracy comprising several nested arrangements that aspire to regulate and represent the human race's economic, social, and security interests. Security Council is the main body with five permanent members and other rotating members. These five permanent members include the UK, China, Russia, the USA, and France, showing the balance of power hidden in the higher echelons of the UN. This has been a double-edged sword as many core and pressing issues slip under the UN's radar due to the veto power of the five permanent members.

The United Nations was created initially to achieve world peace. It was a successor to another similar body named the League of Nations, made to avoid big wars. While the UN was formed to maintain world peace and global instability, its success ratio falls short time and again. The case of the Rwandan genocide in 1994 was one that stands as a question mark for the UN, where it failed, resulting in genocide on a massive scale in the African country. Despite the forces present in the area, the wave of genocide rocked the country, becoming a watershed moment in the nation's history. Another instance in this case is Sudan, which has no resolution. In the same vein, the suffering in Sudan has affected millions of people. Other than that, a more recent case of the UN and its lack of ability to manage a security crisis is the Srebrenica massacre, which involved eight thousand Muslim deaths in 1995, which is a stark reminder of the UN and its inability to maintain peace in regions.

The above instances fully indicate that the UN has failed spectacularly on several occasions in its wholehearted promise of world peace and security. This is mainly due to the permanent five members who often withhold the UN from using the full powers of the international organization on extreme delicacy.

In the same vein, the present condition prevailing in the Middle East between Hamas and Israel has fully exposed the policy loopholes and strength of the US as the lead hegemon at the UN, which often protects Israel from unfriendly resolutions that are passed in the Security Council. Another instance is the war in Iraq that the US and its allies launched against the UN's will, which proves all the institutionalists wrong. Therefore, this stance shows where the power corridors lie, whereas their reach can be pretty much understood while also showcasing the organization's weakness.

International Institutions and Leading States

All the leading international bodies/institutions are the creation of leading states. So, in a way, it can be reasonably assumed that the world powers are primarily responsible for establishing world peace if they have the political will to do so. The world's superpowers can play a massive role in this regard since they are the ones who can promote worldwide peace and security. Therefore, instead of creating bodies like the UN and NATO, which are primarily purposed to create spheres of influence and increase their powers in the international systems. Some concerted efforts occurred when the world joined forces to fight off a common enemy. The instances of global warming, healthcare, and EU environmental policy have allayed some uncertainty. These efforts have been successful in light of pursuing peace and security on the international stage.

On the other hand, the UN has had a considerable share of success in missions like the one in Sierra Leone. Surprisingly, this mission was a massive success since it had the backing of all five permanent members of the UN, resulting in the events that transpired later.

Steps the Governments can Take to Assist the UN

The role of the UN can often only go as far as the governments that can accommodate it. Often, peace is the matter to be decided by the home country and its people, which can then loop in the UN to deliver a new strategy financially and politically that can either work at the state or global level. This strategy can move mountains for the countries and, most importantly, reverse the abysmal record countries have regarding tackling major crises.

The mere step of sustaining peace involves several bodies working inside the UN's ambit, ranging from funds, secretariats, country offices, and programs that join forces in research, planning, and partnerships to further peace and allay conflict. This long-term, holistic approach can encompass human rights, sustainable development, and political mediation. In light of this discussion, listed below are actionable steps the UN and countries can take to enable peace and herald an era of political stability and economic prosperity.

61. Facilitate Trust, Provide Direction, and Enable Accountability

Often, the trust level between the UN and governments weakens. This strategy relies highly on trust for the partnership to work successfully. The countries often provide the UN with competing or unimportant agendas that lack a consistent direction, resulting in counterproductive results. On the other hand, the accountability on UN funding and its outcomes are remarkably low in the same vein as the governments held unaccountable for lack of support of UN and their work.

This issue can be addressed by demanding skilled and experienced UN senior leadership, which can ensure a solid peace agenda that can work consistently. Most importantly, the member states should refrain from influencing appointments and undue political pressure to ensure action and coherent policy while reinvigorating the Peacebuilding Commission, establishing what implies sustaining peace and how to work well with the countries.

62. Give the UN Leeway in Doing its Job

Governments often ask the UN for assistance in conflict resolution but later meddle in its affairs when the UN works on the ground. This is the problem as peace requires merging national processes, which involves host governments' participation in the UN efforts to facilitate active civil society. The World Bank opines that the peacebuilding process can take two to four decades, but the markers of success could be invariably unrealistic and short-term. The countries should understand that peace sustenance can take a few decades and must respect the experience and expertise the UN brings to the table instead of caving into geopolitical or domestic pressures.

As is the case, conflicts have become drawn out and complex, partly due to rising social exclusion, inequality, authoritarianism, and higher competition over resources. Therefore, the UN must innovate to address these challenges. However, the state governments are often reluctant to test the waters with riskier projects. However, risks must be taken to jumpstart pilot projects, scale up the ideas, and apply them cohesively.

63. Resource Allocation at the UN (Pooled and Unearmarked Funds)

Interestingly enough, the UN needs smart money allocation rather than more money. Its peace budget is considerable. For instance, frontline programs had funding for twenty-eight billion in 2015. However, most of this funding was ring-fenced or on a piecemeal basis. The procurement process of the UN takes a lot of time and results in several small projects, making it difficult to scale and coordinate, too. The project also mirrors what the donor wants instead of the UN's.

Evidence shows that properly managed and pooled funds can ensure highly dependable results in comparison. They can work as a platform for strategic coordination, mitigate transaction costs, promote country ownership, encourage mutual accountability, and align funding and strategy. Furthermore, the governments must use the common funds, including the Peacebuilding Fund, to raise the multiyear unearmarked funding and targeted funding to initiate priority programs and raise accountability via streamlined reporting.

64. Empower the UN Politically

The absence of consistent leadership and failure to locate political solutions to pressing crises has undermined the work done by the UN. Interestingly, UN crisis management has the potential to replace political action by governments. As is the case, the UN has the necessary skills and credibility to partake in mediation but is rarely called. Political squabbles engender inaction and put the UN in challenging positions. For instance, it is blamed for the political failings of governments, and in other cases, it seemingly lacks moral authority and ambition, undermining its competency.

Therefore, countries must extend political will and authority to the UN and let it work with the governments and other actors to establish peace and mediate conflict. Priority must be placed on constructive dialogue, and investments should be diverted to mediation capacities and good offices. Doing so can help in political mediation and dialogue that can help circumvent violence and bring about lasting peace.

While the system is somewhat convoluted, the governments must stand behind the Secretary General's vision to revamp the UN structure, culture, and processes while providing the operational, financial, and political backing to achieve the vision for peace and its sustenance.

Alliances Create Neutrality

One can argue that forming alliances helps develop a bipolar status quo in global politics, which can further the efforts made for peace and security. The balance on both sides can often deter the prospect of an all-out war. Scholarly research and conventional wisdom can fully testify that when nations agree on military alliances, they embark on an era of peaceful relations and solid cooperation. For instance, members of NATO would rarely be seen involved in some armed conflict or conflict with others on different matters. In the same vein, countries involved in alliances other than NATO are rarely seen engaged in any armed conflict.

While the military alliance literature focuses more on two countries, the case goes further than that. Alliances can go beyond forming direct connections and tie countries together unimaginably. For instance, creating an alliance between two countries also means the allies of those two countries. Take the case of NATO, which has several members in the organization. All the countries that are a part of NATO are allies, too. Country A is an ally of country B, whereas country C and country D are the allies of countries A and B. Therefore, it is unlikely that countries

A, B, C, and D would ever go out on an all-out war as such since they have a lot in common.

Take the instance of Turkey and Iran, who enjoyed more than a decade of peace (from 1965 to 1979). The two nations were not allied to one another, yet had an alliance with the US. Therefore, the two countries had no military conflicts during this time. However, the advent of the 1979 Iranian Revolution was the moment when Iran broke their ties with the US, breaking ties with Turkey indirectly. Later, Iran and Turkey clashed against each other from 1981 to 2000, leading to helicopter raids and aerial bombings. The allegation from Turkey was that Iran was providing a safe harbor to the militant group on its soil, which was unacceptable to Turkey.

How Fostering Business Can Ensure Peace

This is an alternate method to foster peace since the writing on the wall is pretty clear—spending trillions of dollars on military campaigns is unsustainable, failing to bring peace in any region (many are out there). Therefore, fostering a sound business environment is a method that is under-utilized. Governments may not realize that fostering a business environment necessitates a peaceful political and economic climate free of military and terrorist activities. A sound business environment becomes the hub of thriving businesses where everyone benefits in different shapes and forms. Below are some instances that can be attempted to foster peace and stability in an unstable place.

Economic Activity

The United Nations and World Bank have established correlations between violence and poverty. The general argument is that the presence of jobs and diversification of economic growth and opportunity can help alleviate a region's poverty. Businesses can move mountains in this regard. However, the government can be helpful in this area as it can provide the right infrastructure and ecosystem for businesses to thrive and uplift the community. The transference of tech can upgrade the economies of struggling nations, whereas sound management strategies can further help efficiently run businesses. In the same vein, tech can assist in providing a forum where people of different social parameters can come together to achieve a singular goal. Interestingly enough, Cisco Systems invested ten million dollars in Palestinian programmers and included Israeli people in the same teams. In doing so, Cisco took people and economies that were too distant and reconnected them in person and cyberspace.

65. Rule of Law and International Standards

Instead of taking advantage of a country's power dynamics and higher-ups, companies must abide by the rule of law and respect international labor and environmental standards to promote peace and stability. Mars Incorporated has advocated for

Sustainable Tree Corps and assisted in developing Coca Livelihoods Programs to assess Ghana's cocoa sector, among other regions.

Mars works to raise awareness of the importance of reducing child labor and protecting workers at every level of the cocoa value chain, from the fields to the factories. The company has also committed itself to certifying its cocoa supply as sustainable.

In the same vein, while corruption and violent conflicts can cause rampant instability, businesses with sound ethics and business principles can devise policies that can move the needle in peaceful times. Other rule of law elements that can contribute to peace must include respect for property and contract rights. Further, dispute resolution mechanisms can provide a channel for resolving differences without considering violence as an option. A common instance is that of Mongolia and its tripartite agreement, which the government, civil society, and business representatives signed over. This agreement set up a national mechanism to enable dispute resolution, conflict mitigation, and education regarding mining challenges. This agreement is the first of its kind that stands as a testimony to multistakeholder collaboration regarding circumventing natural resources-based conflicts.

66. Corporate Citizenship

This concept encompasses a wide range of initiatives, extending way beyond the premise of philanthropic activities. The term describes the commitment to ethical behavior in strategy, operations, and culture. As opposed to common assumptions, instead of distracting from maximizing profits, the commitment manifests as a strategic response to market/governance conditions, which can hamper a company's profit margins.

For instance, Coca-Cola has provided pushcarts to female entrepreneurs based in rural Vietnam who are disadvantaged. This enables them to create a separate revenue stream for themselves and makes it easier for Coca-Cola to expand into far-flung areas of the country that are difficult to access via conventional transportation methods.

Interestingly, corporate citizenship can boost communities' environmental, economic, and social health, which benefits these large-scale organizations, who are certainly not immune to whatever happens in their immediate environment. These massive companies can also act as a diplomatic bridge between the US and the countries where they are based.

Even the American government recognizes this effort in their companies. The US Department of State gives the participants an Award for Corporate Excellence to recognize the services of a country in this regard. This award considers the Corporate Social Responsibility (CSR) and other initiatives alongside the degree to which these initiatives are taken. These companies have relationships with external parties in their immediate surroundings.

Conclusion

Creating a better world is not just the responsibility of governments, local bodies, and international bodies. It is also the responsibility of individuals. Not to anyone's surprise, the peace process takes a wealth of time. It begins when we look at our behavior and how we treat others and talk to others around us and outside the country.

It is pretty easy to blame external forces for whatever happened. Playing the victim card comes naturally to many, if not all. This is the time we must take responsibility for ourselves and change this attitude of pointing fingers. Many things can change when every individual takes responsibility for their own actions.

Every leader who once started a war or initiated peace was not a leader. Rather, the leader was influenced by others and ordinary people who had ideas and shared those inflammatory ideas with other decision-makers. This can be used in a different way, as we can influence people's perceptions about war and how they think about it. This can help change people's perceptions about peace. In doing so, they can also shape other's opinions about peace.

About the Author

I am Dr. Oluwafemi 'Femi' Akinkugbe Sr., a product of Nigerian education systems for both my elementary and secondary schooling. I proudly served as a dedicated veteran in the U.S. Army, dedicating a total of 16 years to my military service. Currently, I hold a significant role within the Department of Homeland Security. My academic journey led me to achieve a Bachelor of Science in Computer Science from Tarleton State University. Additionally, I pursued advanced education, earning both an MBA and DBA degrees from the University of Phoenix. In addition to my professional pursuits, I am a devoted born-again Christian, deeply rooted in my faith and love for God. My personal life is blessed with a loving marriage to my wife, Bunmi, and we are proud parents to three wonderful children - Femi Jr., Dami, and Funmi. Beyond my career and family life, I am actively engaged in philanthropy through the Femi Akinkugbe Foundation. Our organization's mission is to foster academic excellence among high school students by organizing challenging and inspiring academic competitions.

www.ingramcontent.com/pod-product-compliance
Lightning Source LLC
Chambersburg PA
CBHW051317120626
46547CB00015B/2270